To Dad   Christmas 09

We love you!

love

the family

D1483500

THE GLENS OF ANTRIM

Landscape Of The Glens – Evolution and Development

ALAN TURNER
FOREWORD BY CAHAL DALLAT

Appletree Press

For Maureen, Lara and Kaye

First published in 2005
by Appletree Press Ltd
The Old Potato Station
14 Howard Street South
Belfast
BT7 1AP

Tel: +44 (0) 28 90 24 30 74
Fax: +44 (0) 28 90 24 67 56
E-mail: reception@appletree.ie
Web Site: www.appletree.ie

A catalogue record for this book is available from the British Library.

The Glens of Antrim

ISBN: 0-86281-980-6

Desk & Marketing Editor: Jean Brown
Additional Editorial Work: Jim Black
Design by Pink Inc Design
Production Manager: Paul McAvoy

9 8 7 6 5 4 3 2 1

AP3294

CONTENTS

FOREWORD

AS A lover of the Glens of Antrim all my life and a keen student of their history, I would always welcome another book about the Glens. I especially welcome Alan Turner's *The Glens of Antrim*, which provides an insight into their landscape and the people who occupied them over the centuries. This splendid text will be of tremendous interest to all admirers of the Glens, as well as providing a useful summary for local historians. Lovers of wildlife will revel in the author's lyrical descriptions of birds ("jackdaws and rooks scallywag across farmland" or "The lonesome, haunting burble of a disturbed curlew"), animals and fish ("sleek salmon surge against a stream in spate").

The book takes us on a long journey through time, from before the nine Glens were first inhabited to the end of the twentieth century. Our route is clearly mapped out by excellent illustrations and photographs, with detailed knowledge of the landscape presented in lucid prose. We share the enthusiasm and expertise of an incredibly well-informed companion and guide.

In his introduction, Alan Turner describes the extended view (to the Scottish mainland and islands, across the Antrim plateau and Lough Neagh to the Sperrins and Donegal, down over Belfast to the Mournes) which forms part of the landscape of the Glens. His book offers a similarly extensive view over the "Glorious Glens" themselves.

Cahal Dallat

Left: From the inside of a derelict house

INTRODUCTION

The voyage of discovery is not in seeking new landscapes but in having new eyes. — MARCEL PROUST

Preamble

IN 1974 as we first dug the garden of our new bungalow in Larne, Maureen, my wife, found two artefacts that were the beginnings of this book. Both finds were taken to the Ulster Museum. One was identified as a fossilised sea urchin in a flint nodule from the Upper Cretaceous Age of about 80 million years ago. The age of the urchin was almost beyond my comprehension, as I had not previously thought in such timescales. The idea that our garden, which stands approximately 100 metres above sea level might have been under the sea, if the fossil was found in situ, was an equally novel concept to me.

Butt End of Stone Axe

The second find was of much more recent origin – a mere four to six thousand years old – but it was even more fascinating. It was the butt end of a polished stone axe, made from the rare porcellanite rock found at Tievebulliagh, near Cushendall. The stone sits comfortably in my palm and it is strangely fulfilling to know this tool was fashioned by a human hand many centuries ago.

Once the axe was identified, I began to read books and articles on Irish archaeology and to visit local sites,

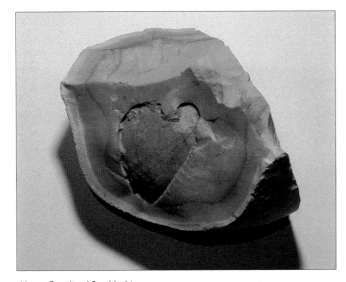

Above: Fossilised Sea-Urchin

Left: Tiveragh from a distance

mainly in the hills. My exploration kindled my love for hill walking and I have since spent many contented days in the Glens on my own and with friends from the Glens of Antrim Rambling Club and Wesley's Walkers.

In my readings I have come across much praise for the beauties of the Glens. For example, Lieutenant Thomas Hore, writing in the *Ordnance Survey Memoirs* in 1833, describes most eloquently what has now become a section of the long-distance trail, the Ulster Way. He writes in a manner with which I can fully empathise, for this is a glorious hike south from Glenarm. "In walking along this line the traveller is well recompensed for any toil he may have endured, by the vast beauties of the scenes all around him. Looking westward he beholds, immediately near him, the surface of mountain on whose summit he stands, undulating and gradually descending for two or three miles to the valley of Glenarm, while in the distance his eye embraces one vast extent of beautiful inland scenery, the most conspicuous object being the mountain of Slemish. Turning to the eastward the scene becomes completely changed. Here if he can turn his eye from the frightful precipice at his feet, he commands a splendid view of the sea, with many parts of Scotland in the distance, as well as the beautiful and varied line of the Irish coast southward, while immediately under him he has the remaining or eastern half of the parishes of Carncastle and Killyglen to the water's edge. From Knockdhu the line of cliffs forms a complete semicircle round the west side of the townland of Sallagh, and are completely lost on its south boundary, giving that townland the comfortable appearance of a well sheltered bay."

The *Ordnance Survey Memoirs* are a source of some excellent descriptions of the Glens. An extract from the report of the Parish of Ardclinis reads: "The drive

Spring Squall

along the coast of this parish is in the highest degree delightful, and is considered the most interesting on the northern coast of this county. From the picturesque promontory of Garron Point, which is perhaps one of the most conspicuous on the coast, nothing can exceed the beauty of the view looking towards the south. The precipitous and beautiful wooded banks which extend along the coast are terminated by the bold headland of Glenarm, beyond which the northern extremity of Island Magee is faintly seen. Towards the west, the range of hills continues along the northern shore and extends up the south east side of the romantic valley of Glenariff. The Scottish coast from the Rinns of Islay to Portpatrick, and some of the distant Scottish mountains are distinctly seen from this coast."

Such landscapes in prose encouraged my search for a greater knowledge of the Glens. When I received early retirement, I decided to integrate my different interests by writing and illustrating with photographs my layman's understanding of how the landscape of the Glens of Antrim evolved and how this region came to be designated "An Area of Outstanding Natural Beauty". This involved studying the rudiments of geology, archaeology, landscape and history as they have influenced the scenery of the region. For those interested I have included an appendix outlining key archaeological methods. It also required many enjoyable walks and drives as I observed and recorded the evidence before me.

The nature of landscape

John Hewitt captured the essence of landscape, as most people understand it, when he composed the following lines in his poem, *Glenariffe and Parkmore:*

"Go to Glenariffe if you'd know this Antrim,
from Waterfoot's wide street of lime-washed walls
with the broad sandbank where the children play
and the gulls cry among the billowy washing.

Go to Glenariffe, take the rising road,
the curving road that hugs the northern slope
that winds and clambers up among the trees
and spreads the little valley flat below:
the corn and grazing trim and limited
by the dark lines of hedges: here and there
the grey gleam of a lane from farm to farm,
the houses white and slated neat as toys:"

Hewitt's poetic landscape is a picture of Glenariff as he experienced it. But that picture is not the one viewed by earlier generations nor is it the view of today. Neither will it remain unchanged in the future.

Ten thousand years ago no human eye viewed the landscape of the Glens and no human hand altered it. That landscape was solely the product of nature. It evolved over many millennia and I will try to picture how nature laid the wonderful foundation for the current landscape. Nature shaped the Glens; man has rearranged its surface.

Roads, forestry, pollution, dams, electricity pylons, houses and fields are illustrative of man's impact on the Glens. We have transformed our inheritance from Nature and the text will explore the many ways we have changed the landscape.

We can see that over lengthy periods of time the landscape alters. However, even in the short term, the landscape is dynamic. While the physical landscape may be relatively constant, its appearance is transient.

The season, the weather, the quality of light, the position of the sun and the shadows it casts contribute to variety in the landscape. Vegetation, the clothes of the landscape, varies in colour and density with the seasons and so dresses the scenery differently throughout the year. Shafts of sunlight on a day of scattered cloud spotlight a field of new-mown hay and shortly thereafter illuminate a different scene. The soft light of early morning sunshine bathes the land in a wondrous glow. Frost or a prolonged drought radically transforms the Garron Plateau so that boots crunch on the usually squishy surface of the bog. A covering of snow on Tievebulliagh adds beauty and majesty to the peak. On days of unrelenting grey rain, moods are grey and the landscape is monotonously grey. Fortunately our weather is rarely consistent and in ringing the changes it alters our perspective of the landscape.

The landscape of the Glens need not be confined by its geographical boundaries. The distant views of regions beyond the Glens add to the diversity and enjoyment of the landscape. On days when haze is dissipated and the extended views are breathtakingly sharp, Goat Fell on Arran and the island of Islay are clearly visible. Walkers on the hilltops can see beyond Cavehill, above Belfast, to the Mountains of Mourne. They can also see Lough Neagh, the Sperrins and the hills of Donegal. Should there be snow, then hitherto unseen ranges of the Scottish mainland appear and the three conical white peaks of the Paps of Jura rise starkly from the dark sea. These extended views are part of the unique landscape of the Glens.

The landscape is influenced by many factors, not least the perspective of the viewer. Each of us sees differently dependant on our experiences.

The Glens of Antrim

The landscape of the northeast of Ireland has a unique and wonderful character. Its charm may be found in the magnificent scenery of the coast road, in Glenariff (Queen of the Glens), in the richness of Murlough Bay, in Rathlin Island and in a host of other locations.

The Antrim Coast and Glens, including the island of Rathlin, were designated an Area of Outstanding Natural Beauty in 1988. The area so designated is referred to in this text as the Glens. The following map identifies the key features of the area, which is just over forty miles from north to south.

Red Bay and Glenariff

We began this Introduction with a quotation from Proust – "The voyage of discovery is not in seeking new landscapes but in having new eyes." May you enjoy a "voyage of discovery" as you read this text.

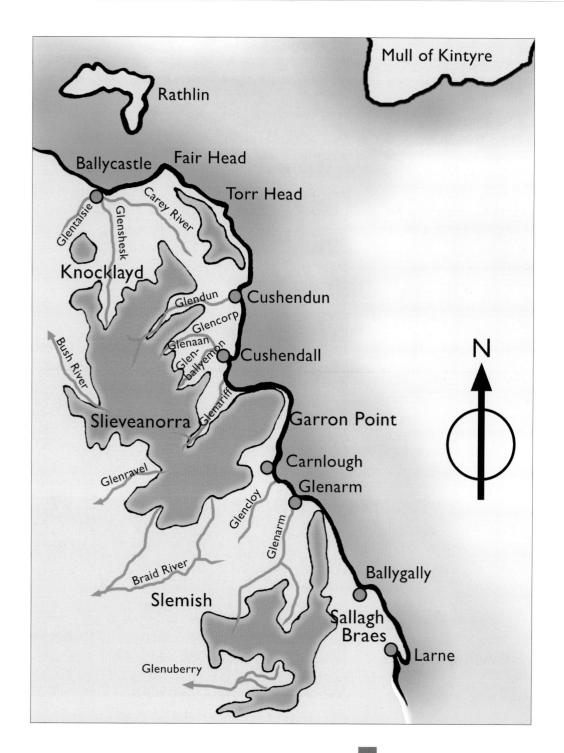

Mull of Kintyre

Rathlin

Ballycastle   Fair Head

Torr Head

Glentaisie

Glenshesk

Carey River

Knocklayd

Glendun   Cushendun

Glencorp

Glenaan

Glen-ballyemon   Cushendall

Bush River

Glenariff

Slieveanorra   Garron Point

N

Glenravel

Carnlough

Glencloy   Glenarm

Glenarm

Braid River

Ballygally

Slemish   Sallagh Braes

Glenuberry   Larne

Harebells

North Antrim Coast from the Fair Head

1. Altahullin Glen
2. Altiffirnan Glen
3. Armoy
4. Ballyvoy
5. Black Rock
6. Brockley
7. Cairncastle
8. Galboly
9. Garron Point
10. Glenariff
11. Glenravel
12. Glenshesk
13. Glentaisie
14. Kilwaughter
15. Loughareema
16. Murlough Bay
17. Red Arch
18. Red Bay
19. Retreat Castle
20. Scawt Hill
21. Slemish
22. Straidkilly
23. The Trosks
24. Tievebulliagh
25. Tiveragh

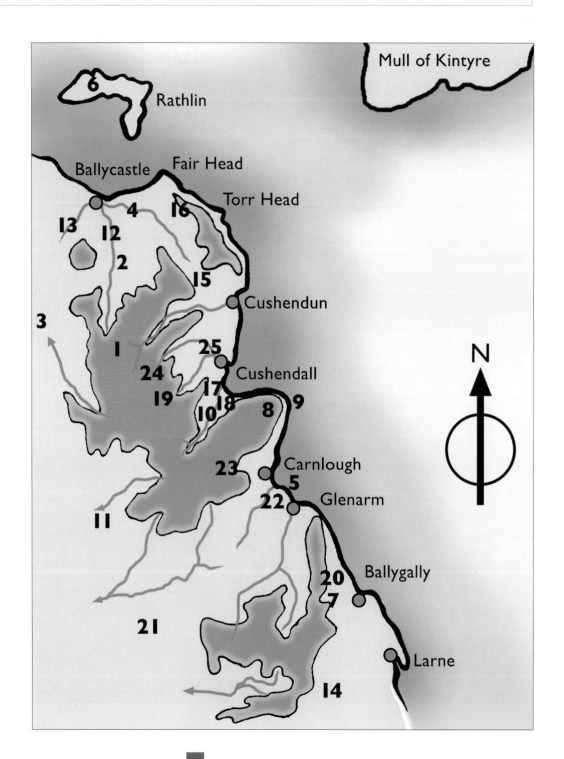

CHAPTER 1

BEFORE MANKIND

"And yet no other corner of this land
offers in shape and colour all I need
for sight to torch the mind with living light."
– JOHN HEWITT, FROM '*THE GLENS*'

A timely perspective

JOHN HEWITT was passionate in his love of the Glens as the foregoing quotation demonstrates but the Glens that he knew took an eternity to fashion. This chapter outlines the evolutionary forces of nature that have helped shape the Glens.

As the old proverb tells us a constant drip wears away stone. We may have to wait a long time, depending on the hardness of the rock and the drip's constancy and force, but no one needs convincing of the rightness of this saying. We know that given time a river shapes its valley. As a dramatic example in the *Ordnance Survey Memoirs* of 1835 the writer notes that in a tributary of the River Dun "stones of more than one ton weight, were washed down by an apparently insignificant stream in a recent inundation." The abrasive power of waves smashes against a cliff and eventually produces shingle and sand. Water infiltrates rock and the resultant chemical reaction, or the cycle of freezing and thawing, shatters the stone asunder. We may not see much evidence of these forces in a single lifetime but we are readily persuaded that water shapes the landscape.

The best example in the Glens of this process can be seen at the base of Fair Head. At this location columns of rock have been broken off by frost and lie in huge piles of block-scree. Professor Charlesworth in his book, *The Geology of Ireland* estimated that some of the blocks at Fair Head could weigh as much as 2,000 tons.

Block-scree at Fair Head

In Ireland we experience floods and gales and know how these can damage the landscape. On television we witness how forest fires, earthquakes, tornadoes, hurricanes and volcanoes alter foreign landscapes. Despite their spectacular and catastrophic short-term effects these forces of unleashed power often result in minimal impact in the long-term shaping of the landscape.

The major changes that form the landscape are not readily observed because human perspective is limited by our lifespan. We see instantaneous and short-term change and if we are observant, and old enough, we notice change taking place over decades. But this is completely inadequate when we consider the evolution of today's landscape. A much longer perspective – several hundreds of millions of years – is needed to appreciate the development of a landscape.

Shore at Lough-na-Crannog

Our experience counts for nothing in understanding the massive changes that preceded the first humans setting foot in Ireland. The first humans inhabited Ireland less than 10,000 years ago yet Ulster's oldest rocks, found between Ballycastle and Cushendun, are over 500 million years old. If we represent the lifespan of this earliest rock as being the equivalent of a 24-hour day, humans have lived in Ulster for less than two and a half seconds!

Dating the rocks

Many sciences have contributed to our understanding of the evolution of geographic Ireland. The evidence is, quite literally, written in stone.

We need first to understand the continuous cycle of the creation, destruction and re-creation of rock. The outer layer of the Earth, mostly under the oceans, is its crust. The crust varies in depth from five to forty kilometres. Immediately below the crust is the Earth's mantle, comprised of semi-molten rock or magma which under certain combinations of heat and pressure becomes liquid. Magma erupts from volcanoes or seeps through weaknesses in the Earth's crust. On losing its gases and cooling slightly the magma becomes lava and this solidifies into igneous rock, the first of the three major categories of rock. The basalts of the Glens are igneous rock.

Sedimentary rock is formed over long periods in two ways. Firstly rivers transport mud and sand, the results of weathering and erosion, to the seabed. Secondly, shells of multitudes of dead sea creatures accumulate on the floor of the ocean. These sediments of sand, mud and shells deepen and solidify into rock either as they are buried under the weight of yet more sediment or as the land rises above sea level and the sediments dry to form rock. Sedimentary rock formed predominantly from layers of shells becomes limestone – common throughout the Glens.

The third major type of rock is metamorphic. This is rock whose form has been changed by heat from the inner layers of the Earth or by pressure when plates collide. The inter-relationships in this continuous process between the three types of rock are summarised in the following diagram designed by Geraldine Gallagher.

It is essential in understanding the evolution of the landscape to be able to date rocks from millions of years ago. One key to determining these dates lies in the uranium that is an element of igneous rock. Uranium is unstable and as it decays at a constant rate it is possible to estimate the age of the igneous rock. Layers of sedimentary rock are dated with reference to over- or underlying strata of igneous rock. It is by this means that geologists have ascertained that the oldest rock in the Glens lies between Ballycastle and Cushendun. At Murlough Bay the relatively recent topmost rocks are almost 500 million years younger than those that are exposed on the southern shore.

The formation of rocks

Weathering, erosion, transportation & deposition

Igneous rock

Metamorphic rock

heat or pressure

heat or pressure

Sedimentary rock

magma

burial & melting in the earth's mantle

A Selection of Rocks on Murlough Beach

Ireland – the wild rover

We learned in school in my days that there are five continents but it was not always so! The crust of the planet is comprised of massive plates that float on the semi-molten mantle. If we observe a liquid as it is heated, there is much activity within the liquid due to

A Fossil from the Antrim Coast

convection. Geologists believe a similar process is at work in the Earth and this causes the plates to move. The plates of the crust have separated and reformed many times and in the process continents have separated and amalgamated.

About 250 million years ago there was only one continent. This landmass slowly divided into the continents that we know today. What is more, they are still moving. America and Europe separated about 180 million years ago. Satellite based measurement systems show that the Atlantic Ocean is widening even if only by a few centimetres each year. (An average movement of 2 centimetres a year is the equivalent of 3,600 kilometres, or 2,250 miles, in 180 million years.) Further confirmation of continental movement may be seen in a map of the Atlantic Ocean. The coast of west Africa and that of south America appear to fit. A study, not of the shorelines, but of the continental shelves, indicates an even closer match. They were once united.

Evidence of the movement of the continents is contained in today's rocks. As igneous rock is formed, there are usually traces of iron oxides within the molten material. These align themselves to the magnetic pole as the rock solidifies. The rock of today contains a permanent record of the direction of the pole at the time the rock was formed. Since the poles remain relatively constant, geologists can demonstrate from the evidence of differing polarities, that the rocks, and therefore the continents, must have changed position.

If continents move, it is no surprise to learn that Ireland, as part of the Eurasian plate, has moved. Five hundred million years ago Ireland was south of the equator at the latitude of South Africa today. Moving steadily north at the rate of a few millimetres per year, it arrived at the equator 350 million years ago. Some evidence of our warmer locations may be found in the fossils from the Antrim coast that could only have originated in tropical seas.

During the movement towards the equator, seasonal rainfall eroded the Irish mountains (the hills of the Glens are the remnants of mountains as high as today's Himalayas) and great rivers transported sand, which accumulated and hardened into sandstone – a sedimentary rock. This Old Red Sandstone may be seen today at Cushendun where it is interlaced with rounded cobbles. This conglomerate is known as pudding stone.

Warm seas containing corals covered the land for 65 million years, and during this period limestone was formed from the debris of shells. Later, when the seas retreated, tropical forest thrived in Ireland. This produced vast quantities of decaying material that would eventually compress to form coal. The mines that were worked at Ballycastle until the middle of the 20th century were created during this period. The fact that coal could not form in our current climatic conditions is further proof that the island has changed position.

The clays of Garron Point contain ammonites, bivalves and belemnites from 250 million years ago. These clays are an unstable base for subsequent overlying rocks and around Garron and north of Ballygally we can see where there are continuing landslips.

At a later stage the climate became exceedingly dry and desert-like. The red sandstone, evident at Red Bay and the Red Arch, is a remnant of the hot desert climate of those long-gone years. Subsequent erosion was most vigorous and much of the coal and sandstone disappeared.

About 150 million years ago Ireland was located at the latitude of southern France. Chalk seas, with abundant tiny-shelled organisms, flooded the land. When the organisms died they accumulated to form sedimentary rock on the seabed. This is the fine-grained white limestone or chalk (readily soluble limestone) that provides the basis for important quarrying activities in Glenarm and Kilwaughter. Chalk covered almost the whole of Ireland to a thickness of 100 metres in places.

Rathlin Limestone

Basalt on Chalk

Silica, a major constituent of igneous rocks, consolidated in the limestone as flint. Flint nodules are readily found in the exposed limestone faces around Glenarm. (Flint was used much later by the first inhabitants of Ireland in the manufacture of tools, such as knives and scrapers, and for creating sparks to ignite fire. An analysis of the distribution of Irish flint tools shows that most were sourced from northeast Ulster.)

Volcanic activity in the Glens

Around 25 million years ago Ireland settled close to its current location. This was near the interface of the European and American plates since the Atlantic Ocean was still in its infancy. (That interface is today deep in the Atlantic but it rises to the surface in Iceland where active volcanoes may be observed.)

Not surprisingly the weaknesses in the Earth's crust at the margins of the tectonic plates resulted in volcanic activity in Ireland – concentrated in the Glens and northeastern Ulster. The molten lava erupted in volcanoes or oozed from fissures to solidify as basalt. This basalt protected the underlying chalk in the Glens whereas in the rest of Ireland the chalk was eroded. The heat of the lava baked the chalk and in the process created unique minerals as at Scawt Hill where scawtite and larnite are found.

The rare substance of porcellanite was formed as the result of the volcanic activity at Tievebulliagh and at Brockley on Rathlin Island. Porcellanite was subsequently used as the raw material to manufacture high quality stone axes.

Tievebulliagh

Evidence of the volcanic activity in the Glens may be seen in Slemish, Tievebulliagh, Brockley, Ballygally Head, Scawt Hill, the Black Rock north of Straidkilly, the Trosks and Tiveragh. Each of these is a volcanic plug that formed when the lava of the vent cooled beneath the Earth's surface. Slemish with a diameter of approximately one-quarter of a mile produced vast quantities of lava. When ice later eroded the mountains, these hard rocks survived as the remnants of the volcanoes.

Slemish

In other places molten lava oozed out and covered the land in great sheets of basalt up to 1,800 metres thick in places (this is approximately five times higher than the highest Antrim hills of today). The Giants' Causeway is a product of this period – its basalt columns are the result of the cooling process of the molten rock. When the flow of basalt was sufficiently deep, similar rock structures (columnar jointing) were created. Examples occur in the Glens at Retreat Castle, the north side of Glenballyeamon, in the rocks above Galboly, on the east coast of Rathlin and at Ballygally Head.

Basalt Columns, Rathlin

At times the lava seeped horizontally into underground weaknesses in the existing rock. When the topmost rock weathered these lava flows, or sills, are exposed. At Fair Head, there is a massive sill over 200 feet deep that now caps the cliffs.

The volcanic activity lasted 15 million years during which there were two major flows of lava. The first flow buried the dense tropical forest. When this basalt weathered and produced soil, there was new growth such as pine, cypress, monkey puzzle and alder trees, as well as ferns. This growth was buried by the second major flow. During this period the formation of deposits of iron ore, as at Glenravel, occurred.

The massive outflows of molten rock in the Glens left voids in the Earth's mantle. These voids encouraged slippage of major portions of rock where large areas sank into the mantle. These are geological faults and they occurred frequently in the Glens. Perhaps the best examples are to be seen when examining the shoreline

The Grey Man's Path

of Rathlin from Ballycastle. We would expect the sedimentary rock, limestone, to be relatively continuous in the horizontal plane. However, there are several sections where breaks in the white limestone are filled by dark basalt. These mark the faults where the limestone now lies below sea level. Indeed Rathlin itself is an isolated part of the Antrim Plateau separated from Ballycastle by a large fault located on the seabed. The Grey Man's Path at Fair Head is a further vivid example of a fault.

'Twixt fire and ice

Fifty million years ago swamp forests with palms proliferated. The climate then began to oscillate between warm and very cold. Tundra reigned during the cold periods and forests flourished in the temperate phases. Peat began to form in this era.

From 25 to 2 million years ago there was a distinct but irregular fall in global temperature. Where the soil was good and the climate moderate, Ireland was densely forested with magnolia, gum trees, palms, redwood, birch, hazel, holly and willow. There were raised bogs, and heather, rhododendron and sphagnum moss grew.

The Ice Age

The fall of global temperatures continued and the first hard frosts in Ireland led to the demise of some of the established plants such as palm trees. During warmer phases of the Ice Age the animals of Ireland included bison, arctic fox, hyena and reindeer. Native Irish mammals of this period were hare, stoat, squirrel, fox, badger, otter and the more exotic pine marten, lemming,

lynx and wild pig (rabbits were introduced later, in Norman times). Wolves, red deer and brown bear also roamed the land and remains of mammoth, dating from 40,000 years ago, have been found near Crumlin. Finds of mammoth teeth and bones have been made on the coast from Larne to Glenariff.

The giant deer, sometimes erroneously known as the Irish elk, was at its peak during this time. The animal was not uniquely Irish, nor was it an elk. The impressive skeleton on display in the National Museum, Dublin, shows what a magnificent creature it was. It stood two metres at the shoulder and three metres to the top of its antlers. The massive antlers had a span of up to three metres and weighed thirty kilograms. The antlers, shed annually, were fragile and not for fighting but to show dominance or to attract females. The giant deer browsed on the plentiful small plants and the lack of predators meant the deer thrived in the prevailing conditions.

From 1.6 million years until about 17,000 years ago the Ice Age prevailed in Ireland. During this period, sometimes free of ice, there were times of intense cold and ice sheets advanced across the sea from Scotland on several occasions. At one stage it is estimated that parts of Ireland lay under ice one mile thick! On one ice advance from Scotland the ice mass surmounted the substantial cliffs of the Antrim coast before invading much further inland. To emphasise the massive impact of this ice, samples of a unique rock from Ailsa Craig, which lies in the Firth of Clyde and is readily seen from the Antrim coast, were deposited in Cork harbour.

Eventually global temperatures rose and the ice gradually melted into the sea. We can see the evidence of the abrasive retreat of an Ice-Age glacier in the U-shaped valley of Glenariff where the ice gouged out the rock to

Glenariff Waterfall

leave steep cliffs on either side. Previous tributaries of the Glenariff River now fall steeply over the cliffs in beautiful waterfalls such as the Mare's Tail.

The flat-topped steep hill at Ballyvoy is the remnant of a glacial delta. The glacial deposits in the lowlands have formed the basis for the good agricultural soils as at Cairncastle in the southern Glens and around Ballycastle in the north.

The meltwater from the glaciers often distributed vast quantities of well-drained sands and gravels as it flowed rapidly in channels under the ice, gushing out when it reached the melting edge. The rock-walled gorges of Altiffirnan and Altahullin Glens are the remnants of glacial drainage channels into Glenshesk. On a smaller scale the evidence of meltwater flows may be seen north of Scawt Hill on the Ulster Way. Some of these became booleyways (explained later) and today often form the highways for quads and tractors accessing the high ground.

The glacial ice in the Irish Sea had been supporting sections of steep cliff as at Garron Point. When the ice melted, the cliffs with their foundations on unstable clays, subsided towards the sea and rotated to lean inland to form a series of platforms. These will continue to slip and erode over the next thousands of years.

A further spectacular remnant of a similar process may be seen at Sallagh Braes where steep inland cliffs form a magnificent amphitheatre of about two kilometres. The debris from this slippage has already been extensively eroded.

Straidkilly (the slipping village) and the uneven surface of the coast road to the east of Fallowvee bear testimony

Sallagh Braes

to the continuing problem of landslips where rocks are based on unstable clays.

The abrasive advances and retreats of the ice reduced mountains of almost 2,000 metres to the hills we know today. In the process the grinding of the ice on rock produced fertile soils for agriculture, sandy deposits at Red Bay and Ballygally beaches and gravel beds around Ballycastle. Deposits left by the melting glaciers diverted rivers. The Bush formerly flowed into Glentaisie but was diverted at right angles at Armoy by glacial debris. Similarly, the Ballyeamon River formerly flowed into Glendun but now flows through Cushendall.
Not only did the ice drastically abrade the landscape, it had other influences. The formation of the ice was due

to an accumulation of snow. The snow originated from evaporation of the seas, so sea levels dropped substantially. On the other hand, the great mass of ice (up to a mile thick) compressed the land like plasticine and this helped to counteract the great fall in sea level. Nonetheless at one stage the coastline was 130 metres below current sea levels. As an illustration of this, peat has been found beneath the sand on the seashore at Carnlough and has been dated to 11,500 years ago.

When the ice eventually retreated, the land decompressed. Since the melting of the ice was relatively speedy compared to the decompression of the land, the sea for a while came further inland and flooded the valleys of the Glens. Hence, we have raised beaches at, for example, Carnlough, where pebbles and shingle lie on the landward side of the coast road. The caves in the cliffs at Red Bay are further evidence of a time when the sea invaded what is currently land.

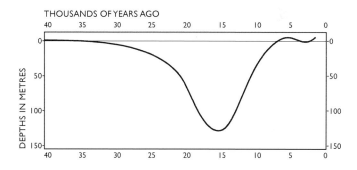

Sea Levels in Metres Over The Last 40,000 Years

We can see from the illustration how sea levels have fluctuated from today's level, which is shown as zero.

This in turn indicates how the coastline has retreated and advanced over that period.

The vanishing lake (Loughareema) is an interesting phenomenon in the Glens. High in the hills the main road from Cushendun to Ballycastle bisects the lake. Sometimes the lake is full, sometimes empty. It fills when the water table is high and drains through a swallow hole when the level of the water table drops. This has been identified as the remnant of an ancient glacial drainage channel. The Glens writer Moria O'Neill wrote of the little lake:

> *"LOUGHAREEMA! Loughareema*
> *Lies so high among the heather;*
> *A little lough, a dark lough,*
> *The wather's black an' deep."*

The end of the Ice Age

Global temperatures fluctuated widely long before there was any suggestion of global warming. Scientists have established that there are cycles of about 100,000 years and within these cycles there are frequent minor cycles of considerable severity. The extreme cold of the last Ice Age ended about 13,000 years ago but there was a significant cold period of about 500 years duration around 10,000 years ago.

The table below illustrates the temperature fluctuations during the period we are now considering. For comparison purposes, mean July temperature in Ireland today is 15 degrees centigrade.

Loughareema

Thousands of years ago	Mean July temperature °C
9	15
10	12
11	9
12	10
13	8

Temperature fluctuations

Thirteen thousand years ago saw the end of the Ice Age. Those plants that survived thrived and there was a massive immigration of new plants and animals over the landbridges that existed between Ireland and Britain. The plants (mostly grass, docks and willow) helped stabilise the gravel and clay soil and thus prevented erosion. The annual decay of these plants added organic matter to the soil and thus enriched it for future plant migration.

The cold snap referred to earlier occurred about 10,600 years ago. Many plants and animals, including the giant deer, disappeared from Ireland. Some limited glaciation returned. Plant cover was incomplete and was composed of arctic species. There was no grass but sage, dock, campions, pinks and chickweed were abundant.

It is believed that the last land connection with Britain was severed about 9,500 years ago when the low-lying land between the two countries was flooded. This halted the migration of plants and mammals and can be clearly seen when we compare the numbers of indigenous species in the table below:

Species	Ireland	Britain
Plants	815	1172
Birds	354	456
Mammals	14	32
Amphibians	2	6
Reptiles	1	4

Indigenous species

The end of an aeon

This chapter has dared to compress a period of 500 million years into a few pages and has merely hinted at the evolution of nature's handiwork on the landscape of the Glens. Until the end of this period, nature reigned and fashioned the region. Molten matter formed the first igneous rocks. The sea flooded the land several times. Rain, wind, tides and rivers eroded the mountains. Volcanoes and lava flows added to the store of rock. Ice ground it down again. The shoreline advanced and retreated. The climate cycled. The overall process has been massive and magnificent. The foundations of what we have come to know as the Glens of Antrim were well laid before man ever set foot in the place.

Landbridges about 14,000 years ago

Landbridges Between Ireland and Britain

Distant Kintyre

Pond with Slemish in the background

Fair Head

CHAPTER 2

HUNTERS AND GATHERERS

The first arrivals

THE FIRST humans in Ireland led a simple life. They depended on skill to catch prey; knowledge of the natural world for collecting Nature's bounty; stout poles and rods for building huts and stone for making tools and weapons. They led a partly nomadic life,

Worked Flints from the Glens

moving on to new territories when food supplies became scarce. They were utterly dependent on what Nature provided and in poor seasons surely went hungry.

Their stone of choice for weapons and tools was flint. They were Stone Age people who lived in the era known as the Middle Stone Age or Mesolithic. The prefix 'meso' indicates middle and 'lithic' identifies that they were users of stone. There is no evidence of Early Stone Age people having lived in Ireland but all of the needs of the Middle Stone Age people were catered for in Ulster. Birds and their eggs, animals, fish, fruit, berries and roots were abundant in season. Trees for building shelters were plentiful as the countryside was widely forested. Most of all, there was an endless supply of flint along the north-east coast.

Flint, when knapped or struck with a hammer stone, produces flakes that provide razor sharp edges for a range of tools and weapons. Flint is an exceedingly durable material, retains its sharpness well and may be retouched when necessary to refresh the edge. Mesolithic man in the Glens used the widely available flint nodules from the seashore to fashion a range of useful tools and weapons.

Where did the first arrivals come from?

As in any spread of population the newcomers came from the nearest adjacent territory. There is some debate about whether man came by a landbridge with Britain or if he came by boat. If man arrived by landbridge it is likely the crossing would have been made from Wales to Leinster as it is believed that this was the last landbridge to survive the rising sea levels. There is no evidence of the outward spread of Mesolithic man from Leinster and thus it is unlikely that a land crossing was made.

Given the perilous nature of crossing the Irish Sea in flimsy boats, it is likely that as short a journey as possible would be selected. If we presume they came by sea, the shortest journey is from the Mull of Kintyre to Fair Head – a distance of less than 20 kilometres.

Archaeologists originally suggested that this was the probable route of the first travellers. Indeed for many years the theory was put forward that the flint content of the white limestone cliffs of Antrim attracted the migrants from the Mull. However, the earliest archaeological finds in Kintyre are from around 6,000 BC whereas Mount Sandel, near Coleraine, was settled one thousand years earlier and so we have to discount this route.

According to the archaeologist Professor Peter Woodman the strongest archaeological connections with Ireland's Mesolithic migrants are to be found in Lancashire, Cumbria and the Galloway area. Thus if a sea journey was chosen, the first crossings may have been from Galloway to Larne – the same route as modern day ferries!

Why make such a perilous journey?

We cannot know for certain but there are various scenarios, as in any migration of population, which may account for this movement.

The population of hunters and gatherers in any location is limited by availability of food, so perhaps the population outgrew its larder. Maybe they were opportunists or adventurers who, having seen the distant shore, decided to set out for a new life. Conflict may have encouraged a movement in population. Whatever the reason, the first inhabitants of Ireland arrived around 9,000 years ago.

The earliest evidence of the Mesolithic in Ireland

It is surprising that the earliest record of man in Ireland is from the River Bann south of Coleraine at Mount Sandel. There must have been settlements (even if short-term) to the east, in areas closer to Britain. Coastal campsites may lie under the sea that today encroaches further inland than in Mesolithic times. Woodman believes that many sites in the Antrim Glens have been obliterated by mudflows. He further points out that many sites have remained undetected or have been deliberately destroyed by mankind. Someday an archaeologist may uncover an earlier site than Mount Sandel and one that lies closer to the east coast of Antrim.

Some of the flint items found at Mount Sandel were of a type not known outside Ireland and Woodman reckoned that it must have taken quite a few generations for such tools to evolve. He concludes that the forebears of the Mount Sandel settlers must have been in Ireland for some time and that there was no contact with makers of flint tools in Britain as the Mount Sandel tools are unique.

Hunting and gathering

When men hunt they require patience, skill, local knowledge and an understanding of the behaviour of their prey. It takes time to learn the skills necessary to be an efficient hunter. The successful Mesolithic hunter was a key contributor to ensuring the continuity of his community and he was, no doubt, held in high esteem by his people.

For several thousand years these earliest settlers hunted the readily available prey. They recognised the importance of conserving viable populations of their quarry as has been demonstrated at English and European sites, where the deer killed were primarily stags. The preservation of the females ensured a population of deer for future years.

In winter, year-old boars were driven out of the herd by mature boars. These young pigs formed part of the diet at Mount Sandel and their culling did minimal damage to the population of wild pigs. The fact that there is evidence of dogs may mean Mesolithic man used these in the hunt. Hares were keenly sought for their flesh and it is likely that they were snared or trapped.

Other mammals known during this period in Ireland were stoat, red squirrel, badger, otter, wild cat and pine marten. In addition, wolf, brown bear, fox and lynx competed with man for some prey and were a possible threat close to any settlement. Ireland did not have any of the wild cattle found through the rest of Europe.

Salmon, trout and eels were caught in rivers. Cod, bass and flounder were taken from the river estuaries or from the seashore. Some salmon was smoked to preserve it, and it is likely that other fish were similarly treated.

Shellfish, crabs and edible seaweed also formed part of the diet.

When fish shoal, as for example at spawning, they present a good opportunity for the hunter. Fish traps and weirs were used to intercept migrating salmon and eels. Spears were used to impale, or clubs to stun, individual fish. Angling was also practised using a small bone point with a cord attached to one end and the other end baited. When a fish took the bait the angler jerked the cord to attempt to wedge the bone point in the fish's mouth. A high degree of skill and luck was essential for the Mesolithic angler to land a fish by this method!

Pigeon, duck, grouse, woodcock, thrush, blackbird and capercaillie were eaten. The goshawk, now extinct in Ireland, was found at Mount Sandel and other sites and it may have been used in falconry. Sea birds were easily captured during their nesting season and they also provided a ready source of eggs.

The bones of animals, fish and birds, sometimes partly burned, have provided much of the evidence of the Mesolithic diet. Some limited proof exists that berries, crab apples, hazelnuts and the seeds of the water lily were eaten. In order to understand how finds of organic materials are analysed please refer to the *Appendix*.

Weapons and tools

Flint is found around the coast of north-east Ulster where the chalk is exposed. The chalk had lain for many thousands of years under massive lava flows and then ice. This compression made the flint nodules difficult to extract from the chalk cliffs. Hence Mesolithic man tended to use flint pebbles which were readily available

Example of Glens Flint Axe

on the beaches at the foot of the cliffs.

Heavy tools such as axes and picks were fashioned from suitably shaped pieces of flint that required the sharpening of one edge or a point. Hammer stones were used to knap the necessary sharpness. The flint axes were small and initially these were hand-held. Later they were hafted (set with handles) but we do not know how this was done. The axes were used for clearing saplings or in shaping wood for house building.

Solid stones, such as quartzite, were used as hammers to knock flakes from flint nodules. The flakes were fashioned into small tools. For example, a flake with a sharp edge and the opposite edge blunted, made a hand-held knife. Differently shaped flakes could become needles, borers, awls, scrapers and spoke shaves. These were useful in butchery, cleaning and stitching hides and basic woodworking.

Even smaller flakes, known as microliths, were used in the earlier part of the Mesolithic era. These fine flakes were mounted in grooved wood to create blades for knives or form barbs for spears and arrows. The hunter with a ready supply of microliths could easily maintain his weapons while on the hunt.

Fragments of wood with evidence of being worked are extremely rare, since they readily decompose, but they do exist. These show that holes were made in wood and grooves cut in shafts to mount microliths. To cut a groove in wood or antler, Mesolithic man used a flint chisel-like tool, called a burin.

In addition to stone and wood, bits of bone were used as points; antlers became picks or harpoons; and animal shoulder blades made ideal shovels. Containers were constructed from birch bark and animal skins. It is likely that baskets of wickerwork were in use. Man in Ireland had not yet learned to make pottery.

Houses

Mesolithic houses were simple affairs as the following photograph of a reconstruction from the History Park, Omagh shows.

A low sod bank provided a circular base about six metres in diameter. On this was constructed a framework of sturdy poles, interlaced with smaller rods. The framework may then have been covered with animal hides or brushwood to provide shelter from the elements. Each house had in its centre a hearth about one metre across. Stake holes, close to hearths, indicate some form of structure for cooking. Each house probably accommodated six to nine people.

Settlements

Food and water were the main determinants of where humans settled. The River Bann, the sea and the surrounding lowlands provided plenty of scope for hunting and gathering at Mount Sandel. Trees, such as Scots pine, birch and hazel, were widely available in any Irish location of this period for firewood, house building, tools and weapons. It is reckoned that most hunting and gathering took place within two hours' walk of a settlement. The settlements were usually in a clearing in the forest. One such site was occupied for several thousand years although this is exceptional. In most cases the sites were either seasonally occupied or occupied until the food supply was depleted.

Specialised campsites for working on flints or for butchering have been found. Some preparatory work on flint nodules and carcasses meant there was less to carry when returning to the settlement. These sites have been identified by the high concentrations of waste materials.

There may have been trading between settlements. For example, it would be convenient for Mount Sandel settlers to gain flint from more easterly settlements by exchanging salmon from the Bann. Some evidence of trading was the find of chert stone (a form of flint) at Mount Sandel. This is likely to have been sourced in the Midlands of Ireland. Given that the prime means of travel was by foot and the country was thickly wooded, this is a quite remarkable find.

Reconstructed Frame of Mesolithic Hut

There is little information on the size of settlements. Some writers suggest about a dozen individuals or several families. Estimates of the total population of Ulster during Mesolithic times range from several hundred to several thousand.

In the settlements children, women and old men would collect locally available fruit and roots, cure and mend hides, maintain the houses, prepare and preserve food and keep the fires burning. The boys would learn the rudiments of hunting from the elders and from the hunters when they returned to camp. This knowledge and the associated skills passed from generation to generation was paramount for the survival of Mesolithic man.

Possible Glens settlements

It is not difficult to identify some prime areas in the Glens which would have been attractive to Mesolithic man. Salmon still return to the rivers at Glenarm, Cushendun and Ballycastle. The earliest evidence of man's existence in the Glens is at Cushendun and this has been dated to 7,500 years ago. Worked flints from the Mesolithic era have been found at Ballygally, Glenarm, Carnlough, Cushendun and Ballycastle. These sites are all by the sea and in sheltered river valleys.

At Bay Farm, Carnlough, a chipping floor dating to 6,500 years ago was uncovered by archaeologists.

Waste flint to a depth of up to ten centimetres was scattered over seven to eight metres. By this date microliths had been abandoned in favour of larger, heftier flint blades. There was no evidence to clarify whether Mesolithic man lived here or merely used the location as a flint factory.

As mentioned earlier it is likely that a wealth of evidence of Glens settlements has been lost forever. Hopefully further sites may yet be uncovered or new techniques in archaeology may reveal missing links.

The Mesolithic landscape

From the arrival of man, the Irish landscape was no longer created and fashioned solely by Nature. Let us be clear though about the balance between Nature's and man's impact on the landscape of the Glens. The foundations of the scenery, that is, the hills, the lakes, the rivers and the cliffs were Nature's handiwork. Man has extensively altered the surface but had little impact on the foundations. Clearing a few trees for settlements was perhaps the most disruption that Mesolithic man inflicted on the landscape over a period of several thousand years from 9,000 to 6,000 years ago.

These first immigrants did not radically alter the land. However, they started a process of change that has continued and accelerated until the present time.

Winter Storm on the Sea of Moyle

1. Ballypatrick Forest
2. Ballyvenaght
3. Breen Wood
4. Brockley
5. Cairnaseggart
6. Carnanmore
7. Dunteige
8. Galboly
9. Garron
10. Garron Plateau
11. Glenariff
12. Knocklayd
13. Loughnatrosk
14. Murlough Bay
15. Nappan
16. Ossian's Grave
17. Ticloy
18. Tievebulliagh
19. Ushet Lough
20. West Torr

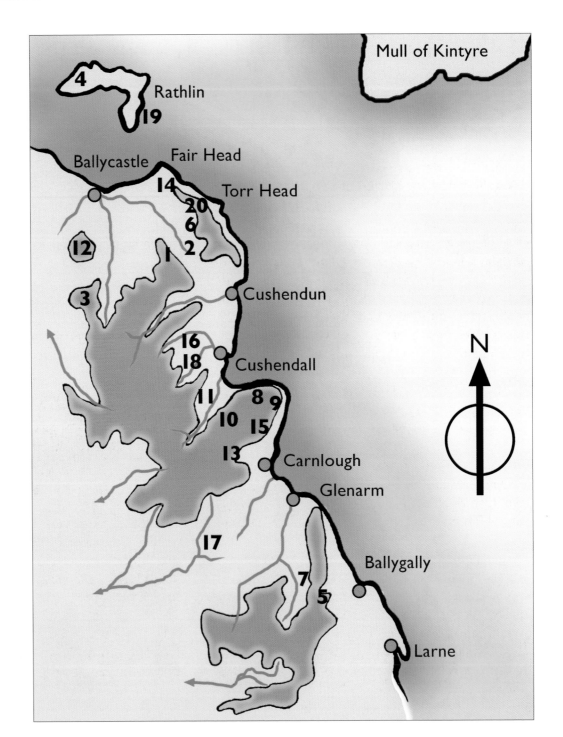

CHAPTER 3

THE INTRODUCTION OF AGRICULTURE

A revolution

MESOLITHIC MAN'S lifestyle and consequently the landscape altered little over the next few thousand years but changes began around 4,200 BC when the first farming communities arrived in the Glens. It is unlikely that individual pioneers could have introduced agriculture since co-operative labour was necessary for success and thus we can infer that communities introduced agriculture. There was, no doubt, some conflict between the newcomers and the resident Mesolithic hunters. In the longer term, however, there was probably a gradual assimilation where the hunters and gatherers learned from the new immigrants and added agriculture to their skills. Neither would the farmers have ignored opportunities to hunt and gather to supplement their farmed produce.

Farmers revolutionised the landscape of Ireland. Initially the change was slow but it was indeed the start of a revolution. From then until today mankind, rather than natural forces, wrought most change to the landscape.

The immigrant farmers were Neolithic (New Stone Age) people who, in order to practice farming, cleared trees to grow grass and crops. Archaeologists, using pollen analysis (outlined in the *Appendix*) found that the tree population began to seriously decline from around 4,200 BC while grasses and herbs thrived. Lest Neolithic man receives all the blame for removing trees from the landscape, he didn't, he only started the process. Trees did not grow extensively on the heights even in these

early times. Pollen analysis of the Neolithic period shows that 80-90% was from trees. One thousand years ago this figure was 30%, while today it is 15%. Now there are scarcely any remnants of original forest apart from isolated examples such as the hazel trees on the steep hillsides of Garron and Glenariff and the oaks of Breen Wood.

The first farmers

Man began to produce food by cultivating cereals and domesticating animals in the Near East over ten thousand years ago. The popularity of this new lifestyle spread across Europe and was brought to Ireland some four thousand years later by the Neolithic immigrants i.e. around 4,000 BC.

Hunter-gatherers lived in the midst of luxuriant growth – most of which was inedible to humans. Wildlife was relatively abundant by today's standards but difficult to catch and those birds that were migratory were only available in season. Gathering of fruits, berries, nuts and birds' eggs was also seasonal, as was the catching of salmon and some coastal fish. Life was precarious due to man's dependence on the environment for providing food.

Farming brought change. An acre of farmed land could provide far more edible calories in the form of grain or domestic animals than an acre of natural forest. Grain was stored for use throughout the year and cattle, sheep, pigs and goats provided meat and milk on a regular basis. Farming was capable of supporting a population ten to one hundred times greater than that of the hunter-gatherers' way of life.

Hunter-gatherer families were constantly on the move. A mother could manage to carry only one child from site to site together with some meagre possessions. Consequently she would not want a subsequent child until the previous one could walk fast enough to keep up with the family. This meant that children were usually spaced at four-year intervals.

Farming led to a more settled existence and mothers could bear and raise as many children as the farm could feed. The norm was to have a child every second year. This, in addition to a more reliable supply of food, led to an increase in population.

The spartan and mobile existence of hunter-gatherers required every able-bodied person to contribute to the acquisition of food. Surpluses were short lived. Farming in settled communities that grew crops and tended livestock led to the creation of surpluses. This wealth creation and subsequent storage enabled a more complex lifestyle to evolve.

Less manpower was required to produce food through agriculture. The excess capacity of labour facilitated the evolution of specialist craftsmen who worked with wood, refined and produced new stone tools, built houses and boats and developed crude pottery. The wealth generated by farming revolutionised the way of life. It eventually led to simple political organisation where a local chief and his family ruled. The chief could afford to have warriors to protect or expand his chiefdom. Priests or druids generated and inculcated

beliefs that in part at least supported the chiefdom. As we shall see later labour was recruited or conscripted for the building of extensive tombs. However all of this lay ahead and we need first to understand the beginnings.

We are certain that the first farmers had to cross from Britain by sea, as there was no longer any landbridge. They not only had to ferry their families but also livestock and the seeds of wheat and barley as these cereals did not occur naturally. It has been suggested that they used substantial skin boats, similar to the curraghs of the west of Ireland, up to 32 feet in length with eight oarsmen and a steersman. Such a craft would be capable of holding two cows and two calves. (Neolithic cattle were only about 125 centimetres high or slightly over four feet.) Alternative loads were ten sheep or goats with two dogs for herding. All the animals would have been trussed for the journey. Pigs were native to Ireland and may have been domesticated earlier.

Stands of elm trees provide evidence of fertile soil and were probably used to locate favourable cultivation sites. The farmers burned swathes of woodland and used the clearance for cultivation and pasture. For a more controlled clearance of trees, ring barking was used. This required a deep gouge to be cut around the bark of a tree to kill off the foliage (and eventually the tree) and let sunlight reach the forest floor. Fire may have been used to clear the undergrowth.

When the nutrients in the soil became exhausted, the clearance was abandoned and trees in another location were removed to start the process again. Thus the Neolithic farmers were what have become known to geographers as "shifting cultivators". The forest gradually reclaimed the original clearing until the land eventually became sufficiently renourished to be attractive for a second clearance. As farming intensified and the population expanded so the tree cover came under increasing pressure.

This was the period when peat began to impact on the landscape. Plants increasingly invaded lakes and ponds until sphagnum moss was established. Alive or dead this moss holds water like a sponge and it traps nutrients. The nutrients in turn release acid and this, with the waterlogging, inhibits the decay of dead plants, which accumulate as peat. This continuing process may be observed as small ponds are gradually infilled. The peat on the Antrim plateau is blanket bog and the lakes there are subject to this process and will eventually disappear.

Cattle, pigs, sheep and goats were the livestock of Neolithic farmers. Their flesh provided food while their hides, skins and fleeces were used for clothing and

Reeds and Bog Cotton on Garron

shelter. Towards the end of the Neolithic period the domesticated horse was introduced to Ireland.

The livestock was probably corralled each night in walled enclosures adjacent to the farmhouses to give protection from predators such as bear, wolf, fox and lynx.

Stone dykes were built to enclose the first fields. These field fences marked boundaries and gave shelter to crops and animals. Traces of such dykes have been found on the Garron Plateau above Galboly, at Nappan and at Loughnatrosk. Many dykes were subsequently buried under peat, and since the peat can be dated using pollen analysis, a minimum age for the stone walls can be obtained. These dates show that the dykes are Neolithic. In the case of Loughnatrosk the peat was dated to 2,300 BC and fields of 200 to 400 metres in width were identified around the lough.

Families would keep herds of cattle to provide meat and milk. Cows past their productive stage, and two- to three-year-old beasts, were the ones usually slaughtered. Unless drying, salting or smoking was used to preserve the meat there would need to have been co-operation between neighbours with regard to the timing of slaughtering and the sharing of the meat. The Neolithic farmers tilled light soils with stone-headed mattocks. The barley and wheat crops they grew provided a staple element of diet. Stone querns were used to grind the grain and three were found by Knowles, the antiquarian, at Ballycastle in 1889.

The rearing of livestock predominated over the growing of crops. This resulted in isolated farmhouses scattered across the countryside, as the farmers needed to be close to their livestock. In contrast, in Europe, houses were built in villages because farming was more oriented towards the growing of crops and farmers chose to live in close contact with each other.

Farming requires a more stable lifestyle than that of the Mesolithic hunters and gatherers. Neolithic houses were accordingly more substantial than those built by Mesolithic man. A reconstruction from the Ulster History Park, Omagh is shown below.

Reconstructed Neolithic House

Houses could be up to six metres square. The walls were built of upright oak planks inserted in trenches. The planks were made by using wedges to split oak trunks. A pitched and thatched roof deflected the rain. Inside there was a hearth and possibly an oven. Smoke escaped by seeping through the thatch.

Neolithic settlements have been discovered at Ballygally and Carnlough. They have also been identified at Ushet Lough in Rathlin and at Murlough Bay. One of the settlements at Carnlough was close to Loughnatrosk at an elevation of 300 metres. This contrasts with Mesolithic settlements that were usually close to the coast or in river valleys. The Neolithic made use of the higher land and practised transhumance, or booleying – grazing their animals on the higher pastures in summer and returning to the low lands in autumn.

Pollen analysis from Loughnatrosk showed that the soil was of better quality three thousand years ago than it is today. It also showed that although the uplands were not extensively forested, hazel, alder and oak grew round the margins of the lough. Not one tree exists around Loughnatrosk today. It is likely that overuse of the land and deterioration in climate brought about the poorer conditions.

Burial modes

The second legacy of the Neolithic era is the wealth of megalithic tombs, remnants of which are still to be found throughout the countryside. (The term megalithic originates in the Greek words for large stones.) Some examples of these huge stone assemblages have remained relatively undisturbed until today. They are usually located 120 to 240 metres above sea level in territory which was suitable for cultivation during Neolithic times.

The Neolithic farmers gave great significance to the marking of at least some individuals' deaths by erecting these massive tombs. It should be noted that the majority of the population was not buried in megaliths. The labour required to haul and erect the immense stones for the megaliths and then to cover the whole edifice with

a mound of earth or small stones, provides proof of a high degree of communal co-operation or perhaps coercion.

Site of Megalithic Tomb

There were four types of megalithic tomb in use in Ulster in the Neolithic period and we will examine each in turn and refer to examples found in the Glens. It is difficult to exactly sequence the four types chronologically but a common order used in archaeological texts has been adopted.

1. Court tombs

Court tombs are also known as horned cairns, court cairns or chambered graves. The variety of names, rather than being confusing, is perhaps helpful in identifying the key features of these graves. They would have had a court (hence the name) in the front of the tomb which may have been used for public ceremonies. The walls surrounding the court gave rise to the term "horns". In the apex of the court is the pillared entrance to the chambers, or galleries, used for burials. The number of galleries in court tombs varies between two and five. The galleries were roofed with flat slabs and then the whole edifice, twenty to thirty metres long, was buried under a mound of earth, or a cairn of stones, depending on which material was more readily available.

The burial was usually in the first or second chamber. There are examples of inhumation (inhumation being the burial of a complete body or the full or partial skeletal remains) and cremation. Bodies may not have been buried immediately after death but placed on a platform and exposed to the elements, as was the practice of some North American natives. The bones may then have been interred in what is termed a secondary burial. Artefacts such as pottery, arrowheads, scrapers, flint flakes, stone axes, stone beads and animal bones are often found in excavations of these tombs. These almost certainly indicate a belief in an after-life.

There are 391 known court tombs in Ireland. These were in use from about 4,000 to 3,000 BC. Most of them are in the northern half of the country and several have been found in the Glens. Lord Antrim of Glenarm excavated one at Cairnaseggart, near Cairncastle, in 1870. The remains of two further court cairns are to be found in Ballypatrick Forest Park.

Ossian's Grave in Glenann is a further example although the name is misleading as the grave pre-dates Ossian (the poet) by several thousand years.

Cairnaseggart Court Cairn

Ossian's Grave

A memorial to John Hewitt has been erected close by Ossian's Grave and it is fitting that the two poets should be commemorated together. Hewitt wrote of his predecessor in his poem, *Ossian's Grave, Lubitavish, County Antrim*:

"The legend has it, Ossian lies
beneath this landmark on the hill,
asleep till Fionn and Oscar rise
to summon his old bardic skill
in hosting their last enterprise."

Hewitt Memorial

2. Portal tombs or dolmens

There have been 174 of these tombs located in Ireland and others have been found in western Britain. Portal tombs have been dated to about 3,500 BC through the use of radio carbon dating of organic material such as bones or remains of camp-fire.

Portal tombs are of a simple box-like construction with two upright stones at the entrance to form the portal and one or more smaller pillars at the rear to support the capstone. In some cases the capstones weighed up to 100 tonnes. As with a court cairn, the edifice was covered with a mound. Those, like the one at Ticloy, that have survived, have long been stripped of their cairns. It is presumed that the coverings were removed by farmers for fresh earth for cultivation or for stone for building walls.

The farmer in whose field the Ticloy dolmen stands has an old photograph of men in stovepipe hats assembled around two dolmens. Unfortunately one of the dolmens has since provided material for a stone wall. The *Ordnance Survey Memoirs* of the 1830s also refer to this second dolmen:

"In the townland of Ticloy...is what appears either a druidical altar or perhaps more probably a tomb formed by masses of rock rudely piled and forming a species of house closed on three sides and at the top. By the people in the neighbourhood it is called the Stone House.

"West of the above site is another, about 20 yards distant. The masses used are not so large as in the other, and those that appear stand about three feet out of the ground. The latter has been much destroyed by the farmer occupying the land having removed some of the stones to help build a fence with."

Two further examples, almost smothered by peat, are in the townland of Ballyvenaght on the eastern edge of

Ballypatrick Forest. These are not marked on the Ordnance Survey map but are to be found at grid reference 201368. One faces east, the other west at opposite ends of a long cairn. It is reckoned that one of these capstones weighs 40 tonnes. There is no clear evidence as to how the massive capstones were raised into place. They may have been jacked up inch by inch or may have been dragged up earthen ramps and the earth later dug away. It is impressive that they still stand today after so many millennia and after their protective mounds have been removed.

Portal Tomb, Ballyvenaght

3. Passage tombs

These tombs are found in Wales, the Orkneys, Portugal, western France and the Mediterranean as well as Ireland. This illustrates the extensiveness of the contacts between Ireland and Europe in those early times. They date from around 3,500 to 2,500 BC. Passage tombs in north Antrim evolved from those in the south of Ireland. Two hundred and twenty-nine have been located in Ireland, the best known being Newgrange on the Boyne. This magnificent and complex structure was erected before the Egyptian pyramids. Usually passage graves are within a circular mound in which there is a stone passage leading to one or a series of chambers. Sometimes the passage is in the form of a cross. The chambers usually have corbelled roofs where each row of flat stones slightly overlaps the row beneath until the opening is completely sealed on a stable base.

With regard to burials, these have been exclusively cremations with a maximum of over one hundred in one tomb. Often there are large stone basins, probably for ritual use, in the passage. Another characteristic of these tombs is the art on some of the massive stones.

There are several examples in the Ballycastle area and in the northern Glens, all situated on heights. One is located on Fair Head, in Cross townland. Other remains are on Knocklayde, West Torr and Carnanmore. An Ordnance Survey pillar disfigures and dishonours this latter monument. Nonetheless Carnanmore is the best example of a passage tomb in the Glens. Situated on high there is a magnificent panorama of Rathlin, Knocklayde, much of the Glens and the Scottish coast. The tomb has little by way of a passage but has a pentagonal chamber 1.5 by 1.2 metres with a corbelled roof and a cairn 22.5 metres across and 4.5 metres high. There are concentric circles and a serpent incised on a roofing slab. Quartz rocks were incorporated in the building of this tomb. Quartz seems to have had desirable qualities for Neolithic man as it was used to face the structure at Newgrange.

Passage tombs, unlike court tombs, had no open area and that suggests a closed ritual. These tombs may have been used for ceremonies where initiates moved through the dark passage into the secrecy of the inner chamber.

4. Wedge tombs

The wedge-shaped tombs have a central gallery for burials. The entrance is via a short antechamber that may be blocked by a stone slab. The whole is roofed with flat stones and surrounded by a further kerb that retains the cairn.

There are 465 wedge tombs in all of Ireland but only a few in County Antrim. There are outline remains of one at Dunteige, near Cairncastle. These tombs were first built in the late Neolithic but they were also used during the subsequent Bronze Age.

Technology and trade

Neolithic man made extensive use of stone for tools and weapons and the flint resources of the Antrim coast continued to be of prime importance. More productive procurement of flint was practised as in the

Dunteige Wedge Tomb

opencast mining at Ballygally Head. Flint arrowheads and javelin points were of a more sophisticated design than that used by Mesolithic man. New activities require new tools and in one such invention flints were imbedded in rows in wood to form the blades of sickles to harvest the cereal crops.

In addition to a more intensive utilisation of flint, Neolithic man searched for other stone raw material. He found and exploited a stone found in only two locations – Tievebulliagh, near Cushendall and Brockley in Rathlin. The site at Tievebulliagh was rediscovered about one hundred years ago and it became the first known Neolithic stone axe-factory in the British Isles. It is probable that the rock was mined by building a fire to heat it and then dousing it with water to fracture the stone.

The blue tinted, grey stone was the result of volcanic activity. The immense heat of the molten lava hardened moist clay, as in the process used in firing porcelain. Hence the geologists named the rock "porcellanite". It is a fine grained rock that may be shaped and polished on sandstone grinding blocks to make excellent quality axe heads. Porcellanite axes are superior to flint in hardness and robustness. They have a sharper and longer-lasting cutting edge. While only the cutting edge needed to be polished in order to be functional, whole axe heads received the treatment. This emphasised the high status of these tools. Woodworking tools, such as adzeheads and chisels, were also made from porcellanite.

Mesolithic flint axes were generally small and suitable only for clearing saplings as they shattered readily on impact with substantial tree trunks. The more robust polished stone axes of Neolithic man have been used in

experiments to fell oaks of up to 35 centimetres in diameter in less than 30 minutes. Pine trees with trunks of 15 centimetres were cut down in less than seven minutes in similar tests.

Porcellanite axe heads were widely distributed in Ireland and Britain as may be seen in the map below.

Some of the porcellanite axes are so huge that it is unlikely they were of practical use for felling trees but may have had a ceremonial purpose. A magnificent

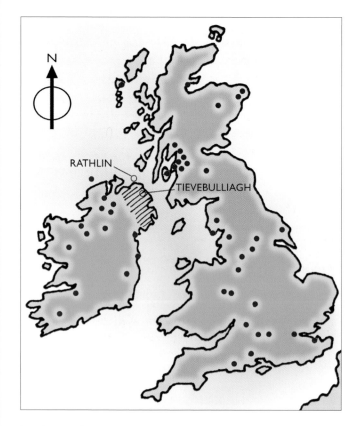

Distribution of porcellanite axeheads

(Area of densest distribution hatched)

hoard of nineteen such axe heads, each up to one foot in length, was found at Malone in Belfast and is on permanent display in the Ulster Museum.

The fragile skin boats continued to ply the Irish Sea, as pitchstone from Arran has been found in the Neolithic site at Ballygally and hoards of Antrim flint have been located in Scotland. Axes of English origin have been found in Ireland and, in particular, one from Cumbria was discovered in Cushendall.

The ceramics of the Neolithic era included crude containers for cooking and storage. The production process probably involved cleaning the clay and adding sand or crushed stone. Coils of clay were then rolled between the hands, just as children roll plasticine. The coils were shaped into a round container and the inside and outside were smoothed with a fine stone. Sometimes impressions of grains of wheat were added as decoration. After drying in the air the pots were fired in a bonfire. The most commonly found pottery in the Glens is known as Goodland. This is named after the townland adjacent to Murlough Bay where fragments of this pottery were first discovered.

The legacy of the Neolithic

The start of the destruction of the natural forest is the main legacy of the Neolithic era. While this facilitated farming and provided many benefits, it began a radical change to the appearance of the landscape. Whether due to successive tree felling alone, or perhaps in combination with changes in the climate, blanket bog began to replace trees in the uplands. Fields, delineated by stone walls, replaced much of the forested lowlands. Mitchell describes the Neolithic countryside as "a mosaic, with areas of virgin forest, tillage patches, rough pastures, and areas of secondary forest in various stages of regeneration." The regeneration of the trees meant that there was still dense forestation in parts of the landscape.

The megalithic tombs are mighty remnants of Neolithic society. These, in their four forms, are relatively abundant in the Glens. They indicate collaborative effort on a large scale and surely have a religious significance.

A third, and less obvious inheritance, is the more sophisticated and settled life style that led to improved technology, including the introduction of pottery. The increase in the population meant a growth in the number of houses in the Neolithic landscape. The isolated farming communities must have collaborated in the construction of megaliths, stone fences, and houses. For example, it is reckoned that 550 hours of communal effort would be necessary to build a Neolithic house. Megalithic graves with capstones of up to 100 tons required the efforts of many people.

Finally there is clear evidence of travel and the interchange of ideas between the peoples of Ireland, Britain and mainland Europe throughout approximately 4,000 years of Neolithic life in Ireland.

Ossian's Grave

Ticloy Dolmen

1. Cairncastle
2. Carn Neill
3. Church Bay
4. Galboly
5. Knockdhu
6. Linford
7. Lurigedan
8. Mullaghsandall
9. Slieveanorra

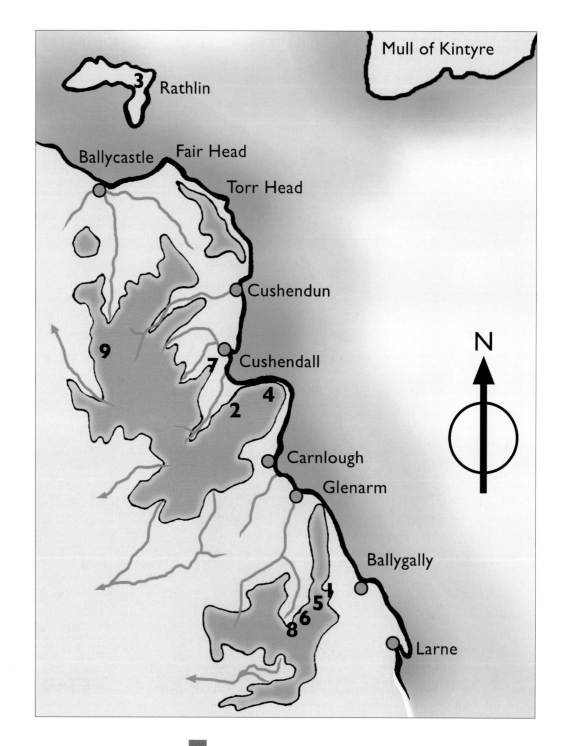

CHAPTER 4

THE METALWORKERS

Further invasions

THE NEOLITHIC people of Ulster may have acquired the skills and knowledge of the Bronze and Iron Ages in the course of trade with Britain and Europe. However it is more likely that invaders brought the new technology. Archaeologists suggest there may have been several major incursions of new settlers in this era which dates from around 2,500 BC to 200 AD.

There is little archaeological evidence of the Bronze or Iron Ages in the Glens of Antrim. This is mainly because the changes are less obvious than the removal of forests, the introduction of agriculture, or the building of impressive tombs. It should however be noted that more spectacular evidence exists in the rest of Ulster. Stone circles, as in the Sperrins, are strangely absent in the northeast apart from one isolated example in the Carnlough hills. Nor has there been any evidence of the rich finds of gold offerings made to the water spirits as at Broighter on the shores of Lough Foyle. The Giant's Ring, near Belfast and the King's Stables and Haughey's Fort in Armagh are prime examples of major developments that seem to have by-passed the Glens.

Technology

Finds of metal tools and weapons, burials and the remnants of field systems are the main sources of our current knowledge of this era in the Glens. Flint continued to be widely used throughout much of the Bronze Age due to the proven capabilities of flint arrowheads, scrapers and knives. Archery kits, comprising of stone wrist guards (known as bracers) and flint arrowheads from the Bronze Age have been found in the Glens. However advances in metalworking eventually led to the replacement of stone by metal in the manufacture of tools and weapons.

Copper was the first metal to be worked. This was cast in open stone moulds to make flat axes. It is remarkable that five hundred of these copper axes have been discovered in Ireland, while only eighty have been located in Britain. Similar axes, known as sisters, because they came out of the same mould, allow us to trace the distribution of axes. Sisters have been found all over Ireland thus showing widespread trading. Many of the sisters are from County Antrim moulds.

Some time after 2,000 BC it was found that tin added to copper resulted in bronze, a more durable metal. Bronze axes were frequently highly decorated and these were probably for ceremonial purposes, as were the earlier polished porcellanite stone axes. Some larger bronze axes were designed as weapons.

The National Museum in Dublin has on display three bronze daggers with blades of about ten, six and three inches that were found on Carrivemurphy mountain (near Carn Neill). A socketed bronze axe from Ballycastle and a bronze spearhead from Cairncastle are also on show. One bronze axe head discovered near Ballycastle, fitted perfectly into a stone mould found at Ballynahinch.

The Bronze Age is renowned for the creation and display of wealth in the form of gold ornamentation. Strips of gold were twisted to form torcs for adornment of neck and wrist. Goldsmiths beat and decorated fine discs. Gold was fashioned into dress fasteners, rings, bracelets, hair ornaments, pins and boxes. Lunulae (collar-like ornaments of beaten gold) are the major gold objects of the Bronze Age in Ireland. These were decorated with rich swirls of Celtic art. They are uniquely Irish. Some were exported to Britain and a few to Europe. Imported amber was used in necklaces. Samples of the rich ornamentation of this period may be seen in the Ulster and the National Museums.

As mentioned earlier, stone moulds for axes have been located in Co. Antrim and provide evidence that metalworking occurred locally. This in turn raises the question from where did they obtain their ores? Copper is found in Cork, Kerry and other southern counties. Tin probably came from Cornwall. There are some suggestions that copper may have been mined in Tyrone and tin in the Mournes but no firm evidence exists. Where did the gold originate? It is known that Slieveanorra (the mountain of gold) in the Glens was a source and the Sperrins in County Tyrone contain gold, but there is no indication of these sources being worked in the Bronze Age. Whatever the sources, there was obviously extensive trading of ores and metals during this period.

The Celts introduced iron across Europe and their skills and knowledge arrived in Ireland around 400 BC. Iron is a harder metal than bronze and therefore more suitable for tools and weapons. Unfortunately iron rusts and eventually disintegrates and thus few artefacts have survived. For example, iron spearheads decayed but the bronze butts that socketed the iron survived.

Iron was more difficult to work than bronze as it required smelting in a furnace, followed by further heating and hammering. However, iron ore was widely available in the Glens.

Agriculture

In Celtic Ireland wealth was amassed in cattle and value was expressed in terms of cattle. For example, six heifers or three milch cows or a female slave were roughly equivalent in value. Cattle were reared mainly for milk and the calves were not killed before six months as they encouraged their mothers to continue to produce milk. Most slaughtering was of animals aged six months to three years. As well as providing milk, meat and hides, cattle provided manure for the crops.

In Celtic times there was no individual ownership of land. Each tribesman could keep and work his land but he could not sell it. If a tribesman wished to sell cattle he had to seek permission from the tribe's assembly. Pliny the Elder, writing in the first century BC, greatly praised the advanced state of Celtic agriculture in Europe when compared with Roman farming. The light ard plough, used until the Early Christian period had required cross-ploughing but the coulter-plough, when it was introduced, enabled heavier soils to be worked as the coulter or blade mounted in front of the ploughshare, cut the roots of plants. Previously unploughed land in the valleys subsequently became arable. The Celts had developed a mobile coulter to fit on their ploughs and this was an advance on the Romans' swing plough. They used manure to fertilise their crops and according to Pliny had developed a harvesting machine which was described as "a big box, the edges armed with teeth and supported by two wheels, which moved through the cornfield, pushed by an ox; the ears of corn were uprooted by the teeth and fell into the box." We have no idea whether such advanced technology spread as far as the Glens but if nothing else it shows the inventiveness and advancement of the Celts.

Prior to 2,000 BC most of the uplands were well drained and wooded. Deforestation made this high ground available for agriculture. However, either the soil became leached through extensive use, without replacement of nutrients by fertiliser, or the climate deteriorated.

At any rate the soil on the hills became water logged, rushes thrived and blanket bog began to extend. Despite the deforestation and the growth of blanket bog, the uplands were not as devoid of woodland as they are today. Remnants of the stumps of pine and oak from those times are found at the base of today's peat.

An increase in arable farming was in part attributable to the introduction of the ard plough. These simple ploughs had only one share with a stone point (later metal) to rip the soil. Pairs of oxen (castrated to ensure

Stumps and Roots on Blanket Bog

a more placid nature when yoked to the plough) dragged the ard to loosen the surface of the soil. A second ploughing at right angles to the first was necessary to fully break the clods. The light ard plough was not

Galboly

capable of working the heavier lowland soils. Despite the increase in tillage, livestock farming of cattle, sheep and pigs predominated. At Galboly Upper there are traces of small stonewalled enclosures where the people would have keep their animals. There are hut circles that are also reckoned to date from the Bronze Age.

The first use of wheels occurred in this period and this led to the development of carts although the use of slide-cars and slipes (low platforms on runners) continued in the Glens until recent times due to the steep hills. The Celts also brought an unusual concept of ownership with regard to land. Each farmer was able to keep and work his tribal land but he could not sell it. He also had to obtain permission from his clan if he wished to sell cattle or other goods.

The Celts increasingly exploited wood as a fuel for heating, cooking and metalworking. It was used in house construction, tool making, fencing and the manufacture of shields and ploughs. The construction of timber trackways (some dating back to 3,500 BC) across bogland was widespread and required much wood as logs or planks were laid side by side on top of brushwood to provide a firm surface. As a result of this activity the forests were being continually depleted.

Burials

From earlier eras we have a rich legacy of tombs in various impressive styles. Each usually contained the remains of several members of the community. In the Bronze Age, individual burials became the norm. The wedge tombs of the late Neolithic period persisted until about 1,200 BC but in the Bronze Age the most frequent burials were single cists (pronounced 'kists'). These are sealed rectangular slab-lined graves built on, or more usually in, the ground and containing single remains. Cists are often grouped in cemeteries. Buried cists are usually unearthed accidentally by farmers ploughing or when builders dig foundations.

A cemetery of seven cists was discovered at Church Bay, Rathlin, in 1983 when gravel was being quarried for enlarging the harbour. The first of these cists was a rectangular box, slightly longer than a metre. In it was the skeleton of a young woman, of about twenty years of age, lying in a crouched position on her side. In five of the other cists similar finds were made, but most unusually the seventh cist contained the remains of five individuals. This cemetery in Rathlin consisted entirely of inhumations whereas cremation was the common means of disposal of the dead in cists discovered elsewhere.

After about 1,200 BC we have little evidence of how communities disposed of corpses. Surprisingly there are many more examples of Neolithic burials than of Iron Age ones. Hoards of valuable tools and weapons have been found in bogs and rivers (but as yet none in the Glens) and these may have been votive gifts to gods. One theory is that human remains were also deposited in these locations where some metal items might survive but organic material would perish.

The simplest monument from the earliest part of the Bronze Age is the standing stone. These may be grave markers or way markers but confusion surrounds such monuments since farmers have in more recent times erected similar stones for their cattle to use as scratching posts! The standing stone on the Mullaghsandall Road was probably a waymarker as it stands clearly on the skyline as it is approached from the south.

Cooking

Wooden cauldrons, of alder or poplar, were used in cooking. The contents were warmed by the addition of hot stones. Riveted bronze sheets were later fashioned into cauldrons and these could be heated directly on a fire. Another unique feature of the Bronze Age is the *fulachta fiadh* or *fulachta fian* (the cooking pit of the deer). These outdoor cooking pits were lined with timber and clay to make them waterproof. The pit was filled with

Standing Stone, Mullaghsandall

water. Large, red-hot stones, roasted on an adjacent fire, were plunged into the water in sufficient quantities to bring it to the boil to cook meat. In a recent experiment a 4.5 kilogram leg of mutton was cooked in four hours by this method.

Inland promontory forts and earthworks

There are fine examples in the Glens of defensive sites from the Iron Age at Lurigedan and Knockdhu. In each case two sides of the hilltop fort required no defence due to steep cliffs. To attack either of the sites from the seaward side would have been difficult due to the extreme gradient of the slopes. Banks (topped with wooden palisades) and ditches protected the inland approach.

Unfortunately we know little of who the defenders and attackers might have been. The forts each cover several acres, so substantial communities and their livestock could have been accommodated but a lack of water, other than rain, in these hill top sites must have created difficulties for any lengthy occupation.

Lurigedan

Knockdhu in Snow

Linford Barrow

There are two fascinating circular earthworks at Linford, west of Knockdhu. There are few similar constructions elsewhere in Ireland and these are the only ones in the Glens. It is not yet clear what purpose these earthworks served. Estimates of their creation range from the first millennium BC to the post-medieval period. It is suggested that in more recent years they were the perfect venue for cock fighting with a ready-made arena and a location on the skyline that made it easy to see the law arriving!

Changes left by the metalworkers

The influx of new peoples and ideas led to trade throughout Ireland and with Britain and Europe as is evidenced in the sourcing of ores and amber. The smiths were receptive to new techniques and the quality of their craftsmanship, as preserved in our museums, was breathtaking. Indeed, this rich gold ornamentation is the key legacy of the period.

Changes in farming were less spectacular. Overall there was an increasing emphasis on stockbreeding and despite the introduction of the ard plough, a decline in cereal growing. Towards the end of the period there was a contraction in arable agriculture and in grassland.

This was the last time that lowland woodland made a significant advance over farmland. In the uplands, the tree cover was never again dominant and the hills became gradually smothered in blanket bog. The importance of cattle in Irish life as a measure of wealth and influence was firmly established.

Sheep Pen

Carnlough from the Coast Road

1. Altagore
2. Ardclinis Church
3. Bonamargy Abbey
4. Bruce's Castle
5. Cairncastle
6. Castle Carra
7. Craigagh Wood
8. Culfeightrin
9. Deer Park Farms
10. Dunteige
11. Glenshesk
12. Glentaisie
13. Layde Church
14. Lough-na-Crannog
15. Orra
16. Red Bay Castle
17. Slemish
18. Tievebulliagh

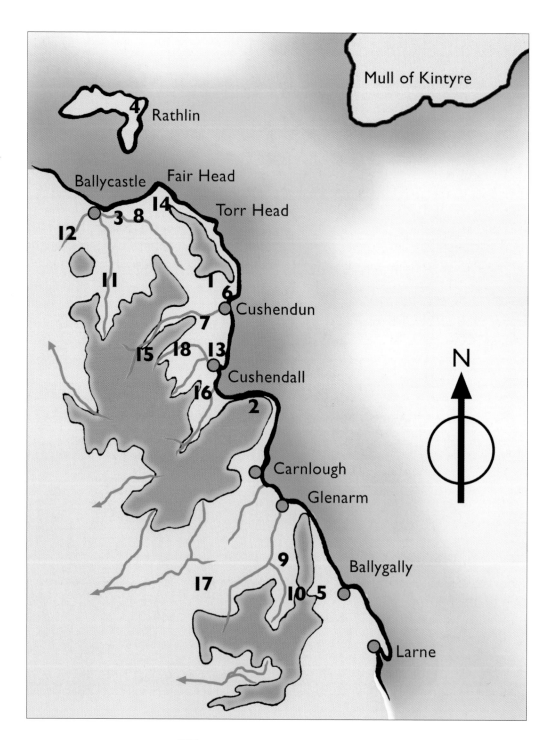

CHAPTER 5

FROM SAINT PATRICK TO THE EARLS OF ANTRIM

Introduction

IN THE previous chapters we have looked at a period of 500 million years from the shaping of the Glens landscape to the lives of Mesolithic and Neolithic man and the influence of the metalworkers.

This takes us to an important divide. From around 200 AD we begin to move from pre-history to a period where an ever-increasing amount of written evidence becomes available. The earliest records from the first century AD were by Romans who had invaded Britain. One named Strabo wrote of Ireland that "the natives are wholly savage and lead a wretched existence because of the cold." Tacitus, another Roman, wrote two centuries later: "In soil and in climate, in the disposition, temper and habits of its population, it differs but little from Britain. We know most of its harbours and approaches, and that through the intercourse of commerce."

Christianity comes to Ireland

Towards the end of the Roman occupation of Britain, when the Romans were distracted by events on mainland Europe, raiders from Ireland took full advantage of the situation. They plundered and took thousands of slaves – one of whom was Patrick, who according to legend herded swine around Slemish.

Religion had been practised in the Glens long before the arrival of Christianity but unfortunately we know little

of its substance. It may have been sorely misrepresented. For example, beliefs and superstitions regarding dolmens featured in an article in the *Dublin Penny Journal* where it was written: "This species of rude altar is very common in many parts of Ireland; it is called both in the Irish and old British language Crom-liagh and Crom-leche, which signify in both a crooked stone, not from any crookedness, but from their inclining posture. They are supposed to have been so formed, in order to allow the blood of the victims slain upon them to run off freely." The article then provides Biblical support (Exodus XX verse 25) for the concept of using unhewn rock in

Standing Stone in Culfeightrin Churchyard

making sacrificial altars. It is unlikely that dolmens were so used, but it is certain that before Christianity men worshipped the sun, moon, stars and planets and also their ancestors. Their burial rites surely had a religious significance; they revered rivers, lakes, wells and springs and invoked their gods' blessings on the harvest.

It is not unusual to find Christians converting holy places, as well as worshippers, to the new religion. The graveyard of the Church of Ireland at Culfeightrin has two tall standing stones that predate Christianity and stand comfortably alongside the headstones of recent years. Bronze Age burials have also been found on this site. Pre-Christian elements have been incorporated in Celtic Christianity to help ease the transition from the former religion.

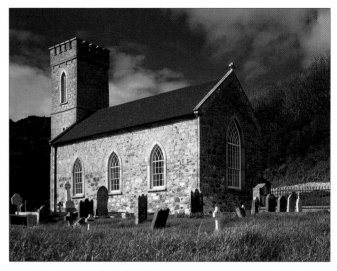

St. Thomas' Church of Ireland, Rathlin

The patron saint of Ireland

Saint Patrick was not the first to bring Christianity to Ireland but it was he who first left a written record of his ministry, which began in 432 AD. Patrick and his fellow missionaries established in Ireland the powerful institution of the organised church.

Although Patrick is reputed to have founded various local churches there is no archaeological evidence of any ecclesiastical site in Ulster before 550 AD. There is stronger evidence that St Comgall, abbot of Bangor, founded a church in Rathlin in 580. The present Church of Ireland, completed in 1823, stands on its site.

The earliest churches were of wicker construction and later built of planks but none of these has survived. It was not until the eighth century that stone churches were built. In 2003 an eight-inch bronze bell shrine

Ardclinis Church

was unearthed near Fair Head. This cover for a sacred bell has a figure of Christ on its front. This most rare find dates to around 1200 AD. A bishop's crozier originating from the ruins of the church at Ardclinis is said to date from the ninth century, but the earliest firm record of the church's existence is around 1300.

Houses and other structures

We have evidence of Neolithic and Mesolithic houses (see earlier chapters) but surprisingly there has been no excavation of a house built in the period between 100 BC and 500 AD. Even in the Early Christian period (500

Reconstructed Rath

to 1100 AD) the only remains that are visible are the masonry and the outlines of drystone-walls. However there has been sufficient research to give a reasonably clear picture of where and how people lived in those times.

Raths (also known as ring forts) were built to provide limited defence to isolated farms and their livestock. The rath was surrounded by a circular bank (occasionally topped with a palisade) and with an external ditch. It is estimated that there are in excess of 30,000 raths in Ireland, most of which date from the Early Christian period. A reconstruction from the Ulster History Park is shown on the previous page.

Cashels served the same purpose as raths but instead of the earthen bank and ditch they had a massive wall. They are found in those areas where stone was plentiful and earth was scarce as at Altagore, to the north of Cushendun.

A rath, 26 metres in diameter, was excavated at Deer Park Farms, Glenarm and provided proof of continual use of the site from the sixth to the tenth centuries. The site was waterlogged and thus many of the remains were preserved. The outlines of about thirty houses were unearthed but probably only three or four stood at any one time in the rath. The round houses, of between 4.5 and 7 metres diameter, had thatched roofs. The walls, comprising two layers of woven hazel rods 30 centimetres apart, were stuffed with moss, grass, straw and heather to provide cavity insulation and then plastered with mud. The sharp ends of the rods always pointed into the cavity to prevent contact with the house's occupants. It has been estimated that eight kilometres of hazel rods were required to construct an average house!

Altagore Cashel

One of the larger wicker houses at Deer Park Farms was joined to another to give a figure-of-eight structure with a connecting aperture. In both of these houses there was a central hearth, well away from the highly combustible walls, and contained within a stone kerb. It is surmised that where such structures existed, the smaller of the two may have been a workshop or a store. In the larger house were two slightly raised platforms of brushwood, covered with finer vegetable material, for use as beds. Timber from one of the doorjambs was from a tree felled in 648 AD.

Souterrains are frequently found in association with raths but were normally built later. It is likely that

Lough-na-Crannog

souterrains were places of refuge although some suggest they were for storage purposes. These underground passages, lined and roofed with stone slabs, are common throughout County Antrim. Entrances were usually well-concealed and steep steps, narrow openings and tight corners restricted movement inside the passages and thus hindered attackers.

Another construction, more defensible than the rath, dating from the Early Christian period, is the crannog, an artificial island. The crannog gets its name from the fact that it was formed by driving the trunks of small trees into the bed of a lake and then infilling the circle with stones and clay. 'Crann' is the Gaelic word for a tree. However the crannog at Lough-na-Crannog at Fair Head was constructed with a surrounding drystone wall, rising to 1.5 metres above the lake, which was infilled with large blocks of granite and topped with a surface of slabs. It was built sometime between 550 and 620 AD.

Most of the houses in Ulster up to 800 or 900 AD were found inside raths. All were round and built as at Deer Park Farms or occasionally in stone. There was a gradual change from round to rectangular houses from 900 AD. These enclosed an area of about 45 square metres – the size of a large room by today's standards but less than half the size of the round houses of Deer Park Farms. Doors were oriented to the south or east to obtain full benefit of the sun and to provide shelter from the prevailing westerly winds. Rectangular houses normally had drystone walls and paved interiors and often had a souterrain with an entrance inside the house. Four massive posts, placed close to the central hearth and well inside the walls, supported the roof. Each long wall had space for seats and beds close to the hearth and the four corners of the house were used for storage. Sometimes wickerwork internal walls were attached to the roof posts to divide the seating and beds from the storage areas. Rectangular houses, unlike their round predecessors, were not confined to raths.

Agriculture

Tenant farmers shared plots of unfenced land for growing crops. To prevent cattle from trampling the crops they were herded for summer grazing to the high ground or booley. The Irish 'buaile' is translated as 'a milking pasture' and the term is preserved, for example, in the names Ballyboley 'the townland of the booleying' and Tievebulliagh 'the hillside of the booley'. The milk from the cows was converted to cheese and butter and buried in the hilltop peat to keep it fresh. The herders stayed all summer with their animals and this annual migration continued until as late as the 19th century.

Most pigs were slaughtered in the autumn when hazelnuts, beechnuts and acorns were no longer available as animal feed. Sheep were mainly kept for wool (pulled not sheared) rather than mutton. (The hills of the Glens are so well suited to sheep grazing that at the time of the outbreak of foot-and-mouth disease in 2001 the Glens had the highest density of sheep anywhere in Europe.)

Fences in the Early Christian period (between 450 AD and 1150) were one of four kinds – a stone wall, a ditch, an oak fence or a post and wattle fence. This last was six feet high with three courses of wickerwork at the top, bottom and in the middle. The posts extended above the wickerwork to allow blackthorn to be interwoven.

Historical landmarks

The kingdom of Dal Riata (also called *Dal Riada*) extending from Bushfoot to Glynn, south of Larne, was the launchpad for the colonisation of western Scotland by the Irish at the end of the fifth century. The Scottish place name Argyll means 'the eastern province of the Gael'. For more than a century this kingdom straddled the North Channel (the Sea of Moyle) and Irish warriors raided as far as the Orkneys and the Isle of Man. The king of Dal Riata, in common with other rulers, gave grants of land to the Church. In such a manner was Iona gifted in 563 AD to Colmcille for the establishment of a monastery that for over two centuries was the most famous centre of Christian learning in the Celtic world.

The Vikings

The period of Irish domination of the North Channel began to crumble from 802 AD when the Vikings first raided Iona. Subsequent raids drove the monks from Iona to establish their monastery in Kells, Co. Meath. One of the monks wrote:

The Vikings raided the rich monasteries of Ireland, established major settlements in Dublin and Limerick, and had a base for a time in Larne. They sailed their longships up the Bann to overwinter several years in Lough Neagh but left little direct impact on the Glens. It was 1014 before they were finally driven out of Ireland. Legend suggests they departed from Ireland from around Garron Point after their defeat at the battle of Clontarf.

The Normans

Inter-tribal rivalry was common in Ireland for many centuries. During one conflict, the Normans were invited to intervene in support of one of the protagonists. The Normans took full advantage of the opportunity and by 1171 controlled most of the south of Ireland. Their use of cavalry and armour gave them a powerful advantage over the less well-equipped Irish forces. The invasion of eastern Ulster by a Norman force led by John de Courcy took place in 1177. De Courcy built his most important castle at Carrickfergus, on the coast south-east of the Glens.

From around the end of the 12th century the Normans erected defensive mottes in strategic locations. Each housed sufficient soldiers to control a local area. Mottes were earthen mounds about 15 metres across and four metres high with a palisade and wooden tower on top. They were frequently built on raths as these provided freely available bases that reduced the construction time. The mottes were placed on key routes and often in line of sight of neighbouring mottes so that visual communication could be maintained. Many mottes are recorded on the Ordnance Survey maps in Norman-controlled territory in the south of the Glens.

Stormy Sea of Moyle

"Bitter is the wind tonight,
It tosses the ocean's wild hair;
Tonight I fear not
The fierce warriors of Norway
Coursing on the Irish Sea."

By the 13th century Glenarm was established as a Norman manor where courts were held. The Normans ruled coastal North Antrim by 1227 and had granted the territory from Larne to Glenarm, as well as Rathlin, to John Bissett, a Norman from Scotland. However, three-quarters of Ulster remained in Gaelic hands as is shown in the following map.

Robert the Bruce (1274-1329) who had suffered many setbacks is said to have spent some time hiding in a cave in Rathlin. While there he watched a spider overcome its many failures in attaching its web. This encouraged him to return to his struggle in Scotland where he at last became king. The remains of Bruce's Castle lie on the east coast of Rathlin above the cliffs where Bruce's Cave is located.

The frequent warring in Ulster often resulted in woodland, crops, homesteads and barns being burned.

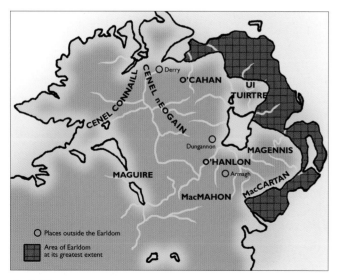

Gaelic Ulster

This destruction intensified on the occasion of Bruce's invasion from Scotland in 1315. For the next thirty years a series of disasters hit Ireland. These included heavy snows, a cattle plague and the death of nearly all the sheep. Following on from that period the weather deteriorated across Europe and agriculture was adversely affected.

Further disaster came as the Black Death swept across Europe in 1348 and 1349 and reduced the population by about one third. This had two effects – more land became available in England and there was less European demand for corn. Thus some Normans found it more attractive to abandon the marginal corn growing land of Ulster in favour of returning to England. The Gaelic lords of Ulster recruited gallowglasses (mercenaries) from the Highlands and Islands of Scotland to harry the Normans and thus encourage this partial withdrawal. The gallowglasses received gifts of land from the local chiefs and they became integrated in the life of the Glens.

The McDonnells

An ancient holed cross at the entrance to the graveyard of Layde Church is said to have been brought from Scotland by the first McDonnells to settle in Cushendall. The Church was in use from 1306 until 1796 and the adjacent Nun's Well may indicate the presence of a nunnery. From such simple beginnings the McDonnells would become one of the most important families in the region.

In 1399 a McDonnell from Scotland married a Bissett of Glenarm and thus inherited the Glens to add to his

Scottish territories. The Sea of Moyle was once again the highway between two parts of an empire. The now powerful McDonnells built Glenarm friary in 1465 but by the 17th century the friary would cease to function. A few remnants of the buildings survive and are on display in the local Church of Ireland. Further waves of Scottish islanders came to the Glens and their family names such as McNeill, McAllister, McAuley and McKay are still much in evidence. Take a look at the entries for McAuley in the telephone directory and you will find a great concentration in and around Cushendall.

Another powerful family in the Glens area was the Irish MacQuillans. One of their members, Rory MacQuillan, built Bonamargy Abbey, a friary of the Franciscan order, around 1500. A blood-thirsty account of how the native Irish responded to the English capture of their Abbey is told in the *Ordnance Survey Memoirs* as follows: "Local tradition says that in some of the excursions made by the English on the coast of Antrim about 1560, they took forcible possession of the abbey...the natives, who were unable to regain their much esteemed edifice by open force of combat...took the alternative of mustering themselves by night on an eminence called Duinnamallaght, a short distance west of the abbey...they heated or reddened iron harrow pins which they fired or discharged against the roof of the abbey which was then, according to the custom of the country, covered with heath. The latter...took fire and consumed the abbey together with the body of Englishmen within its walls, for as soon as the native camp who discharged the fiery arrows found the roof igniting, they instantly repaired to the spot and surrounded the flaming edifice, and by their swords and other weapons kept the doors and windows till nearly the whole of the Englishmen became a prey to the fiery element." From 1616 to about 1639 the friary also served the Scottish islands and Kintyre. Extensive ruins stand on the site south of Ballycastle.

Although a MacQuillan founded the abbey the only known member of the family to be buried there was Julia – the Black Nun. The hole-stone cross in the foreground of the photograph is her memorial.

Black Nun's Grave, Bonamargy Abbey

With two such powerful families in the area it wasn't long before tensions developed and by the early 16th century the McDonnells had fallen out with the McQuillans. In 1558 they fought a major battle on Orra. A simple headstone in Glenshesk marks a McQuillan grave from this battle. The Glens poet James Stoddart Moore recorded the event many years later in verse:

"He fought a hard fight, but he fought it in vain,
MacDonnell has conquered, McQuillan is slain;
Transfixed by a shaft from the host of McCaura
He perished that day on the red field of Aura."

McQuillan's Grave

The McDonnell victory led to the westward extension of their territory into what had been McQuillan's land, right up to the banks of the River Bann. Queen Elizabeth approved of this expansion but was later to have second

Red Bay Castle

thoughts. By the 16th century the Scots had consolidated their hold on the Glens and the English had largely left them alone. However Elizabeth, who was not recognised by the Scots as a legitimate monarch, had designs on controlling the Glens and schemed to dislodge the Scots.

The Gaelic lord, Shane O'Neill had proclaimed himself Earl of Ulster, and he perceived the McDonnells's increased influence as a threat. He had Elizabeth's backing to attack the McDonnells as she too had concerns regarding their sphere of influence. In 1565 with an army of two thousand men, O'Neill marched

down Glenariff and burned Red Bay Castle. Bonfires on Fair Head attracted McDonnell reinforcements from Kintyre but they were late in arriving. In the meantime O'Neill pursued the McDonnells of the Glens and slew 700 of them at Glentaisie. O'Neill's success encouraged him to attack the Pale around Dublin and thus he lost the Queen's support.

Desperate for allies, Shane O'Neill was back in the Glens two years later to seek an alliance with the McDonnells. The hospitality at Castle Carra in Cushendun was initially welcoming but a dispute broke out and O'Neill and his retinue were murdered.

Castle Carra

After 1567 the McDonnells divided their family's interests. James concentrated on Kintyre and Islay while Sorley Boy controlled the Glens and hoped to establish his rights to the Route.

Queen Elizabeth devised a plan to drive the Scots from the Glens and settle English in the territory. In 1575, on the initiation of this plan, Francis Drake, under the command of Essex, helped capture Rathlin and 600 men, women and children were slaughtered. (It is ironic that Church Bay in Rathlin was the final resting-place of *HMS Drake* when she was sunk during World War I.) In the longer run however the campaign failed and the McDonnells made their peace with England. When Sorley Boy recognised Elizabeth as sovereign of Ulster in 1586 he was granted the most fertile half of the Route and by 1620 Randal McDonnell was created Earl of Antrim. At that stage the McDonnells gained the entire Route and owned all the country (300,000 acres) from the northern extremity of Islandmagee to the River Bann, except the priory and monastery of Coleraine.

In 1629 the extensive manorial rights of the Antrim family included fishing, hunting, hawking, all shipwrecks, all waifs and strays, all goods of felons and suicides, holding of courts and the best beast on the death of a tenant. In return the Earl had to have twenty horsemen and 116 footmen armed to support the monarchy. The McDonnells completed a castle at Glenarm in 1636 this was restored in the 1700s and renovated in Victorian times to give today's present structure. The original bridge across the river passed through the Barbican Gate and this gave the occupants of the castle control over who passed north or south.

County Antrim was not subject to the Ulster Plantation

The Barbican Gate, Glenarm Castle

of the early 17th century but the Earl of Antrim adopted the system and invited lowland Scots Presbyterians to settle on his lands. By 1626 twenty-five Scots had been given parcels of land usually of around 150-300 acres. Some of the wealthier immigrant Scots even built tower houses to protect their families. Shaw built such a tower house in Ballygally, now known as Ballygally Castle Hotel, in 1625.

Ballygally Castle Hotel

Cross Incised Stone, Dunteige

The effects of the Plantation on the native Irish were less severe than in the rest of Ulster since the Earl was, at that time, still a Roman Catholic and sympathetic to the plight of the Irish. Nonetheless it appears likely that the Earl taxed his tenants on cows, horses and sheep that grazed on wasteland. Weavers paid a tax and any cow received in dowry required the payment of money to the Earl.

The Penal Laws of the late 17th and 18th centuries were designed to discriminate against Roman Catholics. Parishioners could only worship in secret locations where mass rocks became the altars. A cross-incised stone exists in the townland of Dunteige which may have been a mass rock from these times or simply a standing stone from the Bronze Age which was later Christianised. Another mass rock exists in Craigagh Wood near Cushendun.

The *Ordnance Survey Memoirs* for Cairncastle show that from 1573 to 1610 "the Scots continued to arrive and settle themselves in this parish, and in a very few years became the sole possessors of it." A census of 1659 revealed vast differences in the composition of the population of the Glens. Around Cairncastle over 70% of the population was Scots or English. This percentage dropped dramatically towards the north. Beyond Cushendall less than 10% of the people were of Scottish or English descent. This was the zenith of the influence of the McDonnells. In subsequent centuries they were unfortunate in supporting the losing side in power struggles. Like all the great landlords they faced the erosion of their ownership of vast tracts of land through a succession of Land Acts.

Culfeightrin Old Church

Ruins of Kilwaughter Castle

1. Altnahinch
2. Ardclinis
3. Ballygilbert
4. Bonamargy
5. Braid Valley
6. Bryvore Bridge
7. Carey
8. Cargan
9. Carnalbanagh
10. Carnfunnock
11. Cloghastucan
12. Drain's Bay
13. Drumnagreagh
14. Drumnasole
15. Dungonnell
16. Fallowvee
17. Garron Plateau
18. Garron Tower
19. Glenariff
20. Glenballyeamon
21. Glendun viaduct
22. Kilwaughter
23. Lurigedan
24. Milltown
25. Minnis North
26. Mullaghsandall
27. Murlough Bay
28. Newtown-Crommelin
29. Parkmore
30. Quoile
31. Red Bay
32. Rue Point
33. Sallagh
34. Scawt Hill
35. Skerry Hill
36. Slievenanee
37. The Maidens
38. Turnly's Seat

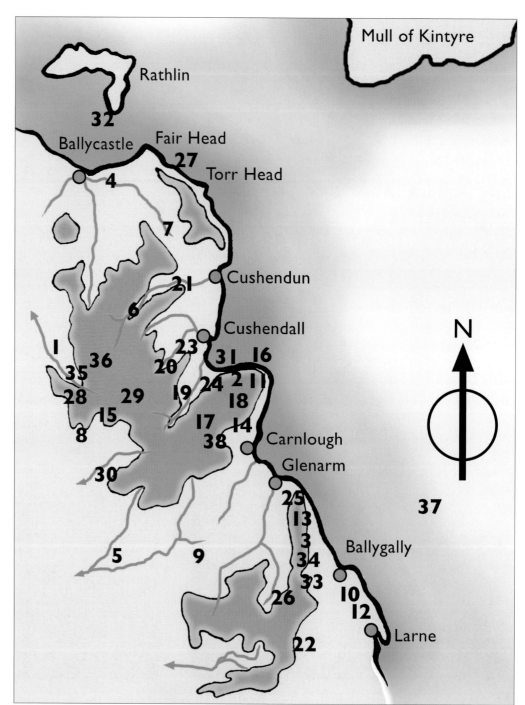

CHAPTER 6

THE INDUSTRIAL AGE TO THE MODERN AGE

IT IS difficult to imagine the hive of activity that once existed in this quiet region since there is scarcely any industry in the Glens today. Current residents usually find employment in Larne, Ballymena, Ballymoney or Belfast but there was a time when coal, iron ore and bauxite mining provided a host of jobs in the Glens and the region even boasted its own railway line.

Industry in the Glens

Coal was mined at Ballycastle and Murlough Bay from at least 1629. Initially the coal was burned in local domestic grates. Later it was used to heat pans to extract salt from seawater on the coast east of Ballycastle and to burn lime for use as a fertiliser. By 1721 the coal was exploited commercially and in the 1750s over 100 miners produced 5,000 to 8,000 tons of coal per year. Coal was shipped to Dublin but with difficulty since Ballycastle harbour could not accommodate sizeable boats.

Hugh Boyd transformed Ballycastle. He began the building of a new harbour in 1737 and he was also responsible for initiating an impressive range of inter-related small-scale industries in the town. He started an ironworks, saltworks, soapworks, a chandlery, a bleachgreen, four tanneries, a glassworks, a pottery and a brewery. The coal, sand, lime and soda for glassmaking were all available locally. The impressive kiln for the glassworks was 60 feet in diameter at the base

and 90 feet high. On the day in 1756 on which Holy Trinity Church was opened for worship Boyd's coffin lay near the altar. He was interred in the vault below the church he had built. The driving force behind this hive of enterprise was lost and industry declined thereafter.

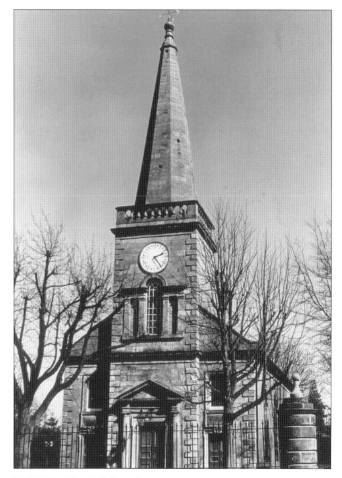

Holy Trinity Church, Ballycastle

Only the coal mining survived, but with diminished output. De Latocnaye, a French nobleman who wrote an account of his walk through Ireland, visited the mines in 1796 and wrote:

"I had the fancy to enter this coal mine, and I went through it to the very end; it is little amusement which, like marriage, one may try once, but I shall not indulge in it again. The mine stretches for about half a mile underground, in a horizontal direction, with sufficient elevation in the line to allow of water flowing away. There is another mine above, and the workers in the two sometimes approach near enough to hear each other working."

By 1967 mining had ceased. Entrances to a few of the mines, remains of a pier and miners' accommodation and the occasional spoil heap, are the only traces left on today's landscape.

Although iron ore was exploited in the Glens during the Iron Age large-scale mining did not begin until the middle of the 19th century. In 1843 Crommelin built a smelting furnace, fired by local peat, in the village that bore his name – Newtown-Crommelin. The local red rock contained 20% iron but the furnace never achieved the necessary sustainable heat and the mining was abandoned.

A more successful enterprise for extracting iron ore was located west of Fair Head (adjacent to the coal mining) in the period between 1850 and 1880. Peak annual production was 30,000 tons. Slievenanee ('Iron Mountain' according to some translations) and the area around Cargan were even more prolific in output, achieving 228,000 tons in the best year. At Cargan the rock yielded 30% iron oxide and 30-40% aluminium oxide. The ore from the Glens was sent to Britain for processing. Spoil heaps and the evidence of opencast workings are all that remain from an industry that ceased operation around 1920.

Iron ore was also mined in Glenarm in the 1860s, at the head of Glenariff from 1873 and on the Garron Plateau in the 1870s. The inclined plane railway that carried the ore from Ardclinis to the quay at Fallowvee has long gone but its route is still clearly visible on the hillside.

Entrance to a Disused Mine on Garron

Bauxite, the raw material for aluminium, was found in the vicinity of the iron ore workings of the Cargan area and was mined from the 1880s until 1933. During the Second World War the increased demand for aluminium for aircraft manufacture led to further bauxite mining on Skerry Hill.

Lime has long been used by the farmers in and around the Glens as fertiliser and in mortar. Defunct limekilns are dotted throughout the landscape. Kilns were built into the hillside to facilitate the top loading of limestone. A fire of coal or peat was lit inside the kiln and alternate layers of fuel and lime were added continuously for several days. The heat reduced the rock to powder. This was spread on the fields to reduce the acidity of the peaty soils and thus improve the yields of grass and grain. Thackeray, who visited the Glens in 1842, wrote: "As one travels up the mountains at night, the kilns may by seen lighted up in the lonely places, and flaring red in the darkness."

Limestone was quarried commercially at Ballycastle, Carnlough and Glenarm from the mid-1800s. From 1854 limestone was exported to Scotland to be used as a flux in the furnaces of the iron industry. Limestone blocks were quarried for the construction industry but mostly the limestone was applied as a fertiliser. Five massive crushing mills to reduce the rock to powder were in operation in Carnlough at one stage. Glenarm and Kilwaughter have surviving quarries and their output is used in agriculture and as a raw material in manufacturing paints, putty, cosmetics, linoleum, toothpaste and flour. Newly-quarried limestone cliffs are brilliant white but with weathering the white

Lime Kiln

Drying Peat

becomes grey and less eye-catching. Thus we find that the massive scars of the abandoned quarries in Carnlough are slowly blending with their environment. The re-colonistation with plantlife speeds the process.

For centuries the domestic fuel of the Glens was peat. The peat was cut by spade from the face of a bank in rectangular turves, stood on end to dry and then drawn home to be built in a stack that provided enough fuel for a household for a year. The labour was intense, so much so, that despite the abundant current supplies, few families now avail of peat.

The peat above Carnlough is rich in sulphate of ammonia and this attracted a German company to mine the peat on the plateau from 1905. A railway on a seven-foot gauge, laid on twelve-foot sleepers, was built across the boggy surface. Trains carried the peat to a continuous-circulation aerial ropeway that was connected to the village. There the peat was processed to produce ammonium sulphate, a nitrogen-rich fertiliser. By 1913 the undertaking was no longer profitable and it closed. The wooden house of the mine manager became a youth hostel but is now derelict. The remains of the three-storey, stone-built accommodation block still exist on the heights, and the bases of the pylons that supported the ropeway may be traced down the valley to Carnlough.

Seaweed (or wrack) has long been used as a fertiliser in the Glens but it also had a commercial use that was exploited from the 1700s. Women collected the weed tossed by the storms onto the shore, and at low tide they waded in the sea to cut further supplies. The wrack was dried and burned in kilns where it became a glutinous mass that was allowed to cool and harden. The product, known as kelp, was then exported for further processing to produce sodium carbonate, potassium carbonate and iodine. Foreign sources began to supply these products more economically and the local trade ceased. The walls of a massive kelp store still stand close to the harbour in Rathlin.

When houses were widely scattered across the countryside and artificial fertilisers and slurry were unknown, fresh water was readily obtained from adjacent streams, wells or springs. The growth of towns and villages led to demand for large supplies of piped water. Reservoirs were built at Quoile, Altnahinch and Dungonnell to meet this demand, mainly emanating from Ballymena and Ballymoney. These reservoirs are the major survivors of the era when the natural resources of the Glens provided employment and sustained local communities.

Communication and transport

Most travel in earlier centuries was on the sea for there were neither good roads nor navigable rivers in the Glens. Until the middle of the 19th century, Kintyre and Islay were more readily reached than Ballymena! Normal mid-19th century trade between the Glens and Scotland involved the export of cattle and lime and the import of ponies and coal. Grain, fish and kelp were shipped to Liverpool, Coleraine and Larne. None of the harbours at Carnlough, Cushendall, Red Bay and Glenarm could easily accommodate boats greater than 20 tons although Cushendun could take craft up to 140 tons. A steamer called in Cushendall once a week on the journey between Larne and Glasgow. In Glenarm, until the lower bridge was built in 1823, small coasters moored alongside warehouses on the river's southern bank. A ferry operated between Cushendun and Kintyre

Cushendun Harbour

from 1709 to 1833.

In the 19th century extensive smuggling of tobacco, spirits, tea and sugar was based on Red Bay and Rathlin despite the introduction of coastguards. Ships from France, Holland and Guernsey were offloaded into small purpose-built local boats of 12 or 16 oars. These were less likely to be detected by the coastguards and they helped maintain a lucrative, if unofficial, trade for many years with Scotland and northwest England.

The coastguard was established in 1822 and cottages for the officers and men were located strategically along the coast at Ballycastle, Torr Head, north of Cushendun, south of Cushendall, Garron Point, Carnlough, Glenarm, Ballygally and Drains Bay. In fact in 1833 the chief officer of the coastguard lived in Ballygally Castle and today, greatly extended, it has been become a hotel. One of the main functions of the coastguards was to prevent smuggling and as we shall see later they were not completely successful in this task! The coastguard cottages are still occupied in some locations but no longer by coastguards.

The lighthouses at the Maidens were built in the 1820s. In Rathlin the East lighthouse was operational from

1856, the West was built in 1912 and Rue Point dates from around the First World War.

Transport by land depended on ponies and horses. In the early 19th century slide cars were used to draw turf from the hilltops. These were described by Dobbs as "composed of two poles, fastened by rungs in the hinder part, on which is placed a wicker creel, about a yard square; having no wheels, it does not press on the ponies which draw it downwards, and it is so light as to be easily drawn up when empty." Slide cars continued to be in service until well into the 20th century.

As we have seen, great mining activity disturbed the tranquil Glens in the late 19th century. The iron ore from the Cargan mines was transported by horse-drawn wagons on a tramway to Parkmore. From there, horses and carts moved the ore down Glenballyeamon to Red Bay. At one stage there were 600 horses at work and the Glens were intensely busy. In 1872 an overhead tramway from Cargan via Glenballyeamon and along the northern slopes of Lurigedan to Red Bay, was built to carry the ore but this was sabotaged a year later. By 1875 a railway line from Ballymena was extended as far as Cargan. This provided more suitable transport for the

The Maidens Lighthouse

ore to the established ports at Larne and Belfast and the horses and carts became redundant.

The ore from the upper reaches of Glenariff was transported on a railway on the south side of the glen to a pier at Milltown. There are few remains of the pier but the pillars of the White Arch bridge stand and a terrace of workers' houses is still occupied.

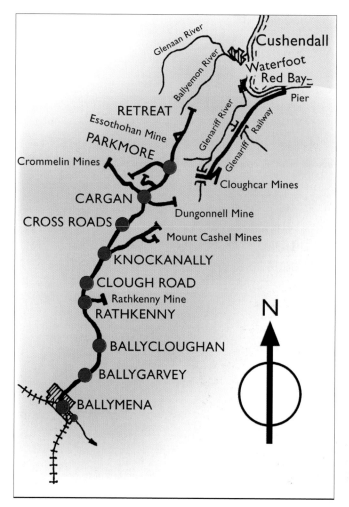

Cushendall and Glenariff Railways

Evolution of the Coast Road

A Norman road once linked the castles of Glenarm and Carrickfergus. It passed below the cliffs at Sallagh and Scawt Hill, rose up to Ballygilbert and to the summit overlooking Drumnagreagh. This latter stretch is now part of the Ulster Way.

The *Ordnance Survey Memoirs* of the 1830s recorded that "The old Ballynure and Glenarm road is a very bad, old, neglected road, the greater half of it in the north being nothing more than a mountain track. It proceeds through the townlands of Sallagh, Ballygilbert and Lisnahay to the summit of the mountain at Drimnagreagh." This was the remnant of the Norman road.

From earliest times there had been a road between Ballycastle and Larne but this was unsuitable for wheeled vehicles, as it was miry and steep in sections such as the Foaran Path at Garron Point and the White Path south of Glenarm. Richard Dobbs in his description of County Antrim in 1683 wrote: "From and by Larne to Glenarm are several highways but none good, for the lower way in winter is very deep, wet clay, and the upper way is great and steep hills. From Glenarm he that would go to Coleraine go either over the mountain to Red Bay, and he must have a guide, or if he go the low way, bad clay ground and deep in winter, he has one hill *[the Foaran Path at Garron]* which is very hard to ride up or down, and the way generally bad, winter or summer. From Red Bay is a very good way to Cushendun, but from there over the mountains of Carey you must have a guide. Another way is lower down in sight of the sea but very great hills, risings and fallings, slippery in winter and steep in summer." The Glenarm River had to be forded at the Castle until the bridge was built to the

Barbican Gate in 1682. The second bridge in Glenarm was erected in 1823. By 1835 a daily mail car plied in each direction between Larne and Ballycastle. An inn at Cloghastucan provided a stable for trace horses to assist wheeled vehicles at the Foaran Path at Garron Point.

At this time there were only two other roads in the Glens – Broughshane to Glenarm and Clough to Cushendall – neither fit for carriages. The Larne to Ballycastle road was improved by Turnly who cut through the Red Arch at Red Bay in 1817 and blasted a headland at Garron Point in 1822 to bypass the Foaran Path. These enhancements were the precursors to the building of the Coast Road in the 1840s.

The building of the Coast Road required vision and it was a magnificent feat of civil engineering. At the southern entrance to the Glens the engineers blasted a tunnel to form the Black Arch but the most striking single feature is surely the magnificent Glendun Viaduct, designed by Charles Lanyon, the architect of Queen's University.

Red Arch

Glendun Viaduct

The Coast Road (a mail-coach road, some say a military road) was being completed in 1842 when Thackeray travelled on it and described it as: "a route highly picturesque and romantic; the sea spreading wide before the spectator's eyes upon one side of the route, the tall cliffs of limestone rising abruptly above him on the other. ...I have seen nothing in Ireland so picturesque as this noble line of coast-scenery."

Coast Road Towards Glenariff

It wasn't long before the Coast Road created an opportunity for the public to view the landscape of the Glens as never before. In addition it impacted on the landscape as it has protected the cliffs from sea erosion by helping to stem the extensive slippage of the coastal hillsides and the mudflows at Minnis North. The bottom of these mudflows would, if left to Nature, overwhelm the Coast Road. On the other hand the protective measures taken to keep the road open lead to a steepening of the slope and this ensures continuing instability.

The new road opened up the Glens to the rest of Ulster. Never again would Scotland be nearer for trading than Ballymena, Ballycastle or Larne. Henry McNeill, a native of Glenarm, saw the potential for tourism and in the late 1800s he began to introduce visitors to the charms of the Glens. Tourists from Scotland and the north of England stayed in his purpose-built hotels in Larne. Horse-drawn coaches carried the tourists on the Coast Road and this was the precursor to the tourist trade that is a mainstay of the economy of the Glens.

Ballycastle's railway, opened in 1880, enabled the town to become a popular seaside resort. Its golf course, opened in 1891, added to its appeal. Francis Turnly, with an eye to encouraging tourism, built the first hotel in the region in Cushendall in the late 19th century. By 1888 a passenger rail service to Parkmore was in operation. The railway company then purchased the land around the waterfalls in Glenariff to provide walkways to attract tourists. The successor to the original teahouse is now a restaurant. A round trip from Belfast by train to Parkmore and then via horse-drawn carriage on the coast road to Larne, from where trains ran to Belfast, was popular, as was the reverse journey.

Larragh Falls

Francis Turnly

Francis Turnly made his fortune in the East India Company and came to live at Drumnasole near Carnlough. He was instrumental in paving a way for the coast road and his name appears several times in the rest of this chapter as he contributed substantially to the development of the area. His name is preserved on the Ordnance Survey map where Turnly's Seat is a rocky prominence on the Garron plateau. This was the place where Turnly could survey much of his land and enjoy a magnificent view. His route to the top took him along the Black Burn. John Hewitt, writing in his poem *The Curfew Tower,* described Turnly's journey as he:

> *"climbed the cliff those waters leap*
> *fern-hung ledge and mossy step*
> *to the hazels near the top,*
> *passed through bracken out to whin*
> *till bog-cotton tufts begin."*

Waterfall on the Black Burn

The invention of the internal combustion engine made the Glens even more accessible to day-trippers and tourists in the 20th century. Hotels, restaurants, caravan parks, self-catering accommodation and bed-and-breakfast establishments increased greatly. Visitors, and those who cater for their needs, have altered the face of the Glens.

Triple Falls on the Black Burn

Turnly's Seat

Houses

The landed gentry and the newly-rich entrepreneurs built grand houses at places like Drumnasole (which Turnly erected around 1840), Kilwaughter Castle (designed by Nash, the architect of the Bath terraces) and Carnfunnock.

On Turnly achieving the summit, Hewitt writes:

*"This high place was his heart's home
here above the waterfall
now the place he loved is still
save for curlew, passing gull."*

Kilwaughter Castle

Another interesting dwelling, the Caves House, was home to Nicholas Crommelin (founder of Newtown Crommelin) from 1847 to 1863. John Masefield, the Poet Laureate, married into the Crommelin family and spent his honeymoon there in 1903.

There was competition to see who could have the most ornate gate lodges, many of which survive. Icehouses, as at Carnfunnock, preserved the freshness of food. Hugh Boyd's icehouse still stands on the sea side of the Ballycastle tennis courts. Exotic trees from foreign parts were planted in the grounds and thus we have some unusual non-native species such as the eucalyptus tree at Garron Tower.

The Irish cottagers lived in much more humble houses built in strictly linear design, never more than one room deep – a restriction determined by the length of roof timbers. If extended, it was added to linearly or it was heightened. Cottages were erected near running water, a well or a spring, in the lee of a hill and with trees for additional shelter. Some cottages were shared with the valuable livestock. These houses were normally built on a slope with the animals in the lower end or on a lower floor to allow manure to flow down the yard!

One of the Many Abandoned Cottages in the Glens

Villages and towns

The mainstay of agriculture in the Glens throughout the centuries has been the raising of livestock. Farmhouses need to be adjacent to the livestock and so houses associated with farming have tended to be

Ice House, Carnfunnock

scattered across the countryside. However, in recent centuries, when a farmer died the law stipulated that the sons of the family inherited the farm as separate units in equal shares. This led to the family's cottages being grouped together in what was known as a 'clachan' and these have provided the basis for many villages. A surviving clachan at Fair Head is now in the possession of the National Trust.

The physical features of the Glens have largely determined the location and growth of villages and towns. Lacking any coastal plain and with much inhospitable upland, most settlements have been in the valleys where the rivers meet the sea. In 1824 Crommelin, ignoring such criteria, planned a model colony (to be named after him) of over 3,000 acres of rough mountain grazing. He invested £14,000 (a considerable sum in those days) but his attempt to create arable land from the hillsides failed probably because as the *Ordnance Survey Memoirs* so succinctly records: "There is only too much water of every kind in this parish." Newtown-Crommelin survives but not quite as its founder planned.

Carnlough, in 1812, was comprised of eleven cabins that were described in the *Memoirs* as "though in general not more than one storey, nor very spacious, are neat and warm, often roughcast and whitened; the windows sashed and the doors painted; covered with a good coat of thatch, and in many instances slated; and with one or two rooms floored." By 1835 Carnlough had expanded to 53 stone houses, mostly thatched. Glenarm was three times as large. Today Carnlough is much larger than Glenarm due to the wide valley of Glencloy that provided space for the expansion of the village. Glenarm is restricted by its steep valley and the boundaries of the Antrim estate.

It was an unusual benefactor, Lady Londonderry (1800-1865), who on the death of her husband implemented their ambitious plans for Carnlough and surrounding area in the 1850s. The limestone quarries, the kilns, the mineral railway to the harbour, the archway over the Coast Road and the harbour were built on behalf of Lady Londonderry. The harbour replaced a dilapidated quay that could only accommodate small vessels of 15 to 20 tons.

Coast Road and Carnlough Harbour

In addition the Londonderry Arms Hotel, a school opposite the hotel, the Town Hall and the coastguard cottages at Garron Point were constructed as part of the overall plan. Earlier, in 1845, Lady Londonderry had built Garron Tower as a rival to Glenarm Castle and also to provide work for those affected by the Famine. The Famine Stone that she had inscribed on the Coast Road reads in part "Unparalleled In the Annals of Human Suffering...when plague and famine stalked along the shore." Lady Londonderry was great-grandmother of Winston Churchill and for a time he owned the Londonderry Arms Hotel.

Londonderry Arms Hotel

On Rathlin in 1837 the majority of the houses were according to the *Memoirs* "of the very poorest description... they are chiefly of one storey, and built of stone – many without a window or chimney, the inhabitants having to be content with the light admitted by the door, and hole made in the roof, by which part only, and that a small portion, of the smoke is carried off."

It is difficult today to envisage anyone buying a complete village but Francis Turnly bought Cushendall in 1810 and made several improvements including building a school and the Curfew Tower whose guardian provided "a place for idlers and rioters".

Curfew Tower

Boyle, in the *Ordnance Survey Memoirs* of 1835 wrote "it is within the last hundred years that Cushendall became entitled to the denomination of a town or village, as about that time it consisted of about six or eight of the most wretched description of cabins which stood in the vicinity of a Mill." However he wrote of the village in 1835 that "it consists of two streets intersecting each other at the centre of the town and contains 113 houses." These houses were built of stone and over half had two storeys.

In the 1830s Cushendun was described in the *Ordnance Survey Memoirs* as follows: "it consists of two parallel rows containing thirteen houses, seven of which are two-storey and slated. They are of a tolerable description. A chief officer and six coastguards occupy three of the two-storey houses. Cushendun is cheerfully situated, and the neighbourhood is frequented in summer by gentlemen's families who have bathing lodges there."

One of the 'bathing lodges' was Rockport Lodge built by Lord O'Neill of Shane's Castle around 1813. From 1874

this was the home of writer Moira O'Neill (real name Agnes 'Nesta' Higginson) and the Lodge was later rented by Louis MacNeice's father as a summer retreat.

Lord Cushendun's wife, Maud, was a Cornish lady and the architect Clough Williams Ellis was asked to design houses in 1925 for building in Cushendall in the Cornish style. These may be viewed in the square and round the corner towards the shore in the Maud Cottages.

Religious discrimination against Presbyterians and Roman Catholics, coupled with poverty and steeply rising rents, led to extensive emigration in the 18th century. The division of farms between sons led to small, uneconomic units and encouraged further emigration.

Deserted Homestead, Mullaghsandall

The Square, Cushendun

The Famine years of 1845-46 impacted on the population of the Glens through death and emigration. This was especially severe in Rathlin where population fell from 1,148 in 1813 to just 453 in 1861: a 60% decline.

Repercussions of famine and emigration may also be seen in the skeletal remains of the homesteads on the marginal farmland in the hills of the Glens. The Glens north of Cushendall lost about a quarter of the population while in the rest there was a decrease of around a fifth.

Increasing farm mechanisation accelerated the decline of the rural population in the 20th century; farm labourers were no longer in demand and they and their families moved to the towns and villages to live and to seek employment.

Agriculture in the Glens

In the centuries before the Famine, as the population increased, there was greater demand for land and so former scrubland was brought into use. In addition more woodland disappeared as farmers sought extra arable land. Lime was increasingly used on heavy soils and farmyard manure, sand and seaweed were applied to the fields. Dobbs, in 1683, wrote that the coastal ground between Larne and Glenarm was good and of deep clay but that it was worn out with ploughing for oats. He observed good feeding for cattle close to Glenarm. Some wheat and barley were grown but no ground was left fallow other than that owned by the Earl of Antrim.

The system of landlords and tenants probably originated in the Bronze Age. When the Normans invaded and became the landlords the majority of tenants were native Irish. These tenants were not allowed to buy land, and what land they held had to be equally divided between sons on the death of the father. This practice, even over a few generations, led to very small holdings that were widely scattered. This system of land-holding, known as rundale, led to the extreme situation in Donegal where half an acre was held by 26 people and in another case one farmer had his small inheritance in 32 locations. The situation was not so dire in the Glens but one Land Agent still wrote, "their townland should be held by four tenants divided into four parcels instead of seventy as before." To help alleviate the problem, Lady Londonderry decreed that if a tenant died, without heir, the immediate neighbour should have first preference to the tenancy in order to consolidate holdings and minimise the number of small plots.

Hill grazing on unfenced rundale was divided according to the acreage of the adjacent land held by the tenants. This determined the number of sheep and/or cattle each farmer could graze. This system has gradually disappeared as farmers agreed on a division of the uplands and then fenced off appropriate portions. Some rundale still exists on Trostan and on the plateau between Carnlough and Glenariff.

There was extensive reorganisation of the rundale system after the Famine and a succession of Land Acts encouraged landlords to sell holdings to their tenants. However it was not until 1904 that the Earl of Antrim sold extensive acreage to his tenants. The photograph of the ladder farms of Glenariff shows how, after reallocation, each farmer received a long rectangular strip of land to include a share of the fertile valley, then the less good land on the lower slopes and finally the poor land on the extreme slopes.

Ladder farms, Glenariff

Sheep and Glenarm Head

The ending of the rundale system encouraged the making of fences. The hedged banks seen today are of recent origin. Most are from the 19th century with only a few going back to the 17th century. The straighter the fence, the more likely it is to be of recent origin. Some of the most pleasing use of drystone fencing is to be found in the vicinity of Carnalbanagh. These walls of rounded stones are holed as open lacework. Their instability is apparent to those who try to climb over and they are unsuitable for cattle unless reinforced with posts and barbed or electrified wire. However they dissipate the wind, shelter the livestock and add to today's landscape.

Vintage Horse Ploughing near Ballycastle

Stone Walls

Those farmers who could afford to own donkeys, ponies or horses recognised their usefulness as means of transportation a well as beasts of burden. They were ridden on and pulled slipes, carts, ploughs, harrows and rollers. The sturdy Cushendall pony was especially suited to pulling slipes with creels of turf on the steep hillsides of the Glens. The ponies were regularly traded between the Glens and Scotland.

The Glens have many streams with a regular flow sufficient to drive waterwheels. From the early 1700s some of the manual labour of farming was replaced by the power generated by the massive wooden water-driven wheels. Threshing, the vigorous action to separate grain from its straw, was performed by threshing mills. Corn mills replaced querns (stone hand mills) in grinding grain to flour or meal. In some cases dairies used waterwheels to power churns. Scutch mills, which separated linen fibre from flax, were in operation in the Glens from the early 1800s. They were mainly in the Braid Valley but were also found in Ballycastle, Cushendun and Cushendall. Several water-powered saw mills were also built. The flat fertile valley of Glenariff frequently flooded, so the river's channel was straightened by a drainage scheme. An Ordnance Survey map of 1904 shows the canal-like river but even today the outline of the original meandering stream may be viewed from Lurigedan.

Spades were used for breaking new ground and for making the inappropriately named lazy beds, more aptly named cultivation plots. The manual labour required was immense. Rows of seaweed, or manure, were first laid along the middle of strips of earth about four feet wide. The soil from either side was dug and piled on top to give a double depth of the thin layer of topsoil. In this bed the peasant farmers planted potatoes or corn. In alternate years the furrows became the ridges. The corduroy pattern of these defunct beds may yet be seen on many of the fields of the Glens. The highest known altitude for lazy beds is at a site near Bryvore Bridge on the banks of the Glendun River at 250 metres above sea level.

In 1835 the main crops in the Glens were potatoes, wheat, oats and beans with the occasional crops of barley, rye and flax. Hay was harvested by scything, until reapers came on the market in the 1850s. Grain crops were cut with reaping hooks and sickles; the stalks were bound in sheaves and stood in stooks to dry. The first mechanical reaper-binder appeared in 1884. Somewhat earlier, in 1871, threshing machines began to replace flails.

Vintage Threshing, Cushendall

An extract from Hewitt's poem *The Thresher* captures the event well:

> *"So the busy man on the top of the stack*
> *Tosses the sheaves with a steady throw,*
> *And none of his mates has a minute to slack*
> *As the bales run out in an endless row,*
> *And the clean grain bulges the open sack*
> *And chaff drifts round like a golden snow."*

In the middle of the 20th century farmers tended to self-sufficiency by growing a range of crops and keeping a variety of livestock and poultry. At the start of the 21st century specialisation has become predominant. The small farms, small fields, scattered holdings and difficult terrain of the Glens do not lend themselves to modern industrial-style cultivation and so many farmers in the region now concentrate on sheep and cattle. Only 3.2% of the lowland Glens are cultivated. As a result many farmers earn a second income in other occupations.

Forestry

Two thousand years ago species such as ash and poplar were more available than oak or elm. There probably were managed woods as timber and rods were necessary for construction; and nuts and fruit were valuable for

Curious Sheep

Lone Tree at Murlough

Over half the trees on Glenariff's western slopes today are hazel and the rest is mostly a mixture of hawthorn, birch, willow and rowan or mountain ash.

The most common trees of today are the Sitka spruces that have been planted extensively from the second half of the 20th century. These fast growing trees are mainly to be found in State-managed forests. Current policy encourages the planting of deciduous trees and a few Glens farmers have small plantations in fields that were formerly grazed. However one tree in a Cairncastle graveyard has a more exotic past. Remnants of the Spanish Armada foundered on the Antrim coast in 1588 and it is told that a Spaniard from that fleet was buried in St Patrick's Church, Cairncastle. He happened to have a Spanish chestnut in his pocket and this is said to be the origin of the fine tree in the graveyard.

human and animal diets. Trees were classified by law according to their value. High value trees were yew (dense wood for high-quality carpentry), oak and hazel (for their nuts and timber), ash (for the making of spear shafts) and pine (for building).

Apart from recent afforestation no trees grow today on the open hilltops of the Antrim plateau. However there are well-weathered stumps and root systems apparent where the peat has been eroded and in the deep black pools of the mountain burns. The hilltop bogs were on average three to nine feet deep but in places up to 25 feet. In the *Ordnance Survey Memoirs* of the 1830s it was reported that trunks of fir and oak trees (primarily the former) were sometimes found in the bog. In Glenariff, the surveyors uncovered oak trees up to three feet in diameter which had their trunks broken off from the roots. The trunks were lying with their heads towards the sea. What awesome force came down the glen to demolish these sturdy trees?

By the mid-19th century a few scattered remnants of the natural woods stood in Breen Wood, Glenariff and around Garron Point. Some reports suggested Glenariff had been forested from cliff to cliff prior to this date.

Cairncastle Tree

Fishing

The sea has long provided a harvest to the Glens people. Plentiful herring shoals passed each May and June. Sole, turbot, flounder and plaice were readily netted on the sandy bottom of Red Bay in the mid-18th century while cod and ling were taken in deeper waters. Whiting, pollan, lobsters and crab provided excellent fishing at Cushendall and Cushendun in the same period. Mackerel, lythe and glashen were also taken off the coast of the Glens.

Wild salmon, waiting for a favourable flood to enter their home streams, splash impatiently in the estuaries. The netting of the annual runs of salmon has been practised for centuries at Ballycastle, Torr Head, Cushendun, Cushendall, Carnlough and Glenarm. Icehouses were built at Ballycastle and Torr Head to store ice until the summer's catch was ready for packing. Dobbs wrote in 1683 that the sea around Glenarm contains plenty of fish "but the people are in no way industrious to take them." We may question Dobbs's views but it is worth noting that even today that few fishing boats operate from the Glens' harbours yet other boats and occasionally factory ships are seen in the coastal waters.

The outside world

The two World Wars of the 20th century devastated many countries but fortunately had little direct impact on the Glens. Rathlin was the most affected region

Working Boat

because of its strategic position in the North Channel. Ships out of Glasgow and Liverpool were targets for German submarines and much naval action took place close to Rathlin.

During the First World War a fleet of drifters maintained a series of wire nets between Kintyre and Rathlin to impede the U-boats. Normal shipping was directed to pass between Rathlin and Fair Head and it was at this time that Rue Point lighthouse became operational while the other two lights on the island were kept out of use.

There were many naval encounters in the waters around Rathlin during both Wars and wrecks litter the seabed. The most famous loss was in 1917 when the heavy cruiser *HMS Drake* was torpedoed off Rathlin. She limped round Rue Point to an anchorage in Church Bay but was so badly damaged she sank. Her resting-place is marked with a large buoy just outside the harbour.

Even the two World Wars of the 20th century had little permanent impact on the coastal landscape of the region. Small groups of headstones in Bonamargy and Rathlin mark the graves of sailors – known and unknown – who lost their lives off the Antrim coast and are buried far from home. Other tombstones and memorials to locals who died in foreign fields exist but little else has left its mark on the landscape.

The Glens have tended to be a quiet haven with the events of the outside world having little impact. Ballycastle on the northern extremity is the only sizeable centre. Despite the advantage of having hosted some of the earliest inhabitants of Ireland, the Glens has a limited population. This is primarily due to the minimal amount of fertile farmland – much of the territory is too high or too boggy. The lack of a strong agricultural base had hindered economic growth. The physical boundaries provided by the deep valleys and steep hills compounded this lack of development, as there were no decent roads until recent centuries to join the region with its hinterland. The links with Scotland that thrived in earlier times were no substitute for connections with the rest of Ireland. Another barrier to economic development of the Glens has been the lack of substantial natural resources.

While all of these economic handicaps have hindered the growth of the population they have generally preserved the uniqueness of the landscape – the solitude of the heights, the unspoiled beauties of the glens and coast and the pace and quality of life in the Glens owe their existence to the relative isolation of the region for many millennia.

War Graves at Bonamargy

Sundial, Carnfunnock Country Park

Riverside Walk, Glenarm

1. Agnew's Hill
2. Ballypatrick Forest
3. Breen Wood
4. Cairncastle
5. Carn Neill
6. Carnfunnock
7. Garron
8. Garron Plateau
9. Glenariff
10. Glencloy
11. Glenshesk
12. Knockdhu
13. Knocklayd
14. Loughareema
15. Lurigedan
16. Newtown-Crommelin
17. Sallagh
18. Tievebulliagh

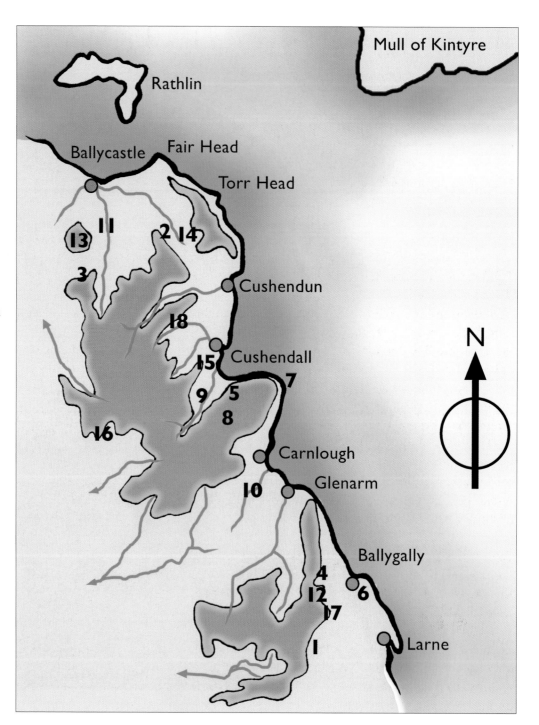

CHAPTER 7

THE NATURE OF TODAY'S GLENS

The peaceful and romantic valley of Glenariff, bounded on either side by lofty and precipitous hills surmounted by a wall of basalt and partially wooded, has not rival in the north in wildness or beauty.
– JAMES BOYLE, *ORDNANCE SURVEY MEMOIRS*, 1830-38.

PREVIOUS CHAPTERS have explained how the Glens have evolved and how Ireland the island moved from the southern to the northern hemisphere and for long periods was under the sea. We have considered the outflow of lava in northeast Ulster; the deep sheets of ice that covered the land and reduced mountains to hills and the many ways Nature laid the foundations of the landscape. We have examined how mankind has interacted with the surface of the landscape through the clearance of trees; the spread and influence of farming; the building of megaliths, churches, houses and roads; and the commercial extraction of natural resources. This gives a surface view of events, a snapshot of the landscape's evolution.

The detail of the living landscape is its wildlife, flora and fauna. The landscape throbs with life. Farmers cut hay, shepherds tend flocks, tourists photograph views and fishermen lift lobster pots. We can readily witness these and a myriad of human activities. The wildlife, an important contributor to the living landscape, doesn't always seem so accessible but there is an abundance of wildlife to be found along the coast, in the valleys and on the hilltops. An observer, with time, patience and some knowledge will find a wealth of birds, mammals and plants in the Glens of Antrim.

The birds and animals

One of the treasures of the Glens is the variety of birds that enlivens the landscape. Jackdaws and rooks scallywag across farmland in a stiff March breeze and bring life and vivacity to the scene. What is more joyous and uplifting than the lilting of the first skylark of Spring high above its heathery haunts? The charm of goldfinches adds brightness to any day as does the glimpse of the bright yellow belly of a grey wagtail as it flies over a bridge to follow the course of a mountain

After a Spring Squall

stream. These birds form but a sample of the bird population.

The coastal waters and rocky shores are haunts of eider, mallard and shelduck. Oystercatchers, in their black and white plumage, probe the seaside turf with strong red beaks. The lonesome, haunting burble of a disturbed curlew does not interrupt the busy foraging of redshanks at the water's edge. Statuesque cormorants with outstretched wings perch on rocky islets to dry their plumage. Gannets from Ailsa Craig soar over the coastal waters. One veers slightly and reveals its brilliant white feathers and stark black wing tips. It carefully folds its wings and plunges into the sea in a surprise attack. Fulmars, with their stiff winged flight, abound on the cliffs south of Glenarm. During the nesting season

guillemots and razorbills crowd the seastacks at the West Lighthouse of Rathlin and it is here that the occasional puffin may be seen.

Ravens cronk in the remote hills and, during their winter courtship, perform masterful aerobatics when they engage claws and cartwheel through the air. Grouse, reared by local gun clubs, settle in the deep heather and rise with a great flurry when intruders approach too close. Unfortunately, the corncrake is no longer heard in the Glens nor are there any choughs remaining on the Fair Head cliffs or in Rathlin. The yellowhammer is increasingly rare.

It is most pleasurable to walk the banks of the many gurgling, splashing mountain streams of the Glens. Small trout frequent these and are prey to the lone

Ducks and Seals on the Rathlin Coast with Torr Head in the Distance.

heron that stands patiently poised to strike. A dipper in white waistcoat flies with fast wing beats along the

Quiet Waters Running By

stream to a favourite rock that is bespeckled with the evidence of previous perchings. Sleek salmon surge against streams as they swim upstream to their spawning redds.

Sightings of birds of prey are infrequent but patience and careful observation, together with an element of luck, bring rewards. I have sighted peregrines and buzzards in coast, glen and hilltop. I have watched peregrines, with only slight twitches of feathers, use the uplift of air above a cliff to retain a fixed position in the sky. One August I was mesmerised by parent peregrines and three fledglings indulging themselves in such an air current. They launched into the updraught to be lifted high in the sky and flew back time after time, to continue their exuberant and exhilarating flying lesson. On another occasion when searching for fossils on the seashore, I had the unanticipated, and rare, bonus of seeing a peregrine pass food to its mate in mid-air.

Kestrels, hovering with their fan tails outspread, are relatively common. On the other hand sparrowhawks are not so readily seen, yet once I drove for several miles on a quiet country road behind an oblivious hunter as it flushed the verges for prey. The circling glide of buzzards in a thermal is a not unusual sight in the Glens. Their beautiful, speckled plumage is seen to full effect when the sunlight catches them during a swoop.

The hen harriers of the Glens form a unique sub-specie. They have taken to nesting in the trees of conifer plantations, unlike birds of the main species that nest on the ground of the moors. It is a delight to watch the V-shaped wings of a harrier as it drifts over its heathery haunts and makes an occasional predatory dive to the ground.

Merlins may be seen perched on fence posts at the edges of conifer forests but these spectacular yet tiny birds of prey are best viewed in the air where one can appreciate their manoeuvrability.

The most abundant mammal is the rabbit. Prey for the buzzard, it is also targeted by foxes that may occasionally be seen loping along an escarpment or dodging through ferns. I was fortunate one June evening to watch a vixen and her two cubs at play on a ledge of the cliffs at Knockdhu. Dusk is also the best time to observe badgers at their setts although I saw two youngsters romping in the Country Park at Carnfunnock early one morning.

Otters are rarely sighted. Sadly, the first one I ever saw, I probably killed. As I drove south from Carnlough on a dark winter's evening, the otter darted across the road from the seashore. I could not avoid it. No trace of the creature could be seen – I hope it survived. My second sighting was also the victim of a traffic accident. With great difficulty it managed to drag itself over the rocky foreshore at Carnfunnock but once in the water it swam freely. Several years later I witnessed two otters swim vigorously along the coast at Carnfunnock and I couldn't help wondering if they were the offspring of the injured one.

Frogs of varying hues of green and brown hop in the mossy uplands. Their spawn is less plentiful than in previous years but the ditches above Glenariff are filled with the jellied eggs in springtime. Lizards are infrequently seen but I once came across one sunning itself on the step of an Ulster Way stile. Occasional red squirrels inhabit Glenariff, Glenarm, Glencloy and the slopes of Garron.

Mountain hares have been trapped in the Glens for pitting against greyhounds in coursing but thankfully some escape the nets to grace the hills. This practice is not as widespread as it once was. Rarely do mountain hares turn completely white in winter but I observed one such near Slemish several years ago. One year I watched seven hares sporting in a hillside field – racing wildly, suddenly switching direction, pausing while they reared up to survey the scene and then "haring" around the rough grassland once more.

Feral goats live on the cliffs of Glenariff, Glenarm, Garron and Agnew's Hill as well as in the upper reaches of Glenshesk. Even if not seen, their pungent aroma is often enough evidence of their presence.

Offshore seals show their curiosity by poking their heads out of the water to gaze all around. The greatest concentrations of seals are the colonies of the grey or Atlantic seals on Rathlin and the Maidens, where they

Seals in the May Sunshine

haul themselves out to bask on the rocky shoreline. In the month of May I have seen sixty seals in one colony on Rathlin. These seals grow as large as 9-10 feet and weigh over 600 lbs. They delight in basking on the rocks at the water's edge and may be approached quietly until they no longer feel secure, at which stage they slip their massive bodies into the sea where their graceful movements contrast with the clumsiness they display on land.

The flowers

Nature's seasonal handiwork colours the Glens with wonderful splashes. Primrose banks adorn the coast road and bluebells carpet the hills below the cliffs at Sallagh. Roadside verges display celandines and dandelions. There are stands of yellow iris, russet ferns in winter, flowering thorns that brighten the hedgerows, red clusters of rowan and hawthorn berries, fuchsia hedges of the coast and wild orchids in Rathlin but most evident of all is the dazzling gold and dark green of the gorse. This vibrant, prickly plant emblazons the hillsides and embellishes the Glens. The hedges of the Glens provide a haven for birds, animals, insects and plants and the white blossom of hawthorn and blackthorn give the green countryside even more spring colour. Thankfully there has not been extensive bulldozing of these beautiful boundaries.

Bluebells

Celandine

Ferns

Primroses

Orchids

The best of the Glens – A personal view

A location which must feature on any such list of the region is Rathlin Island. Its coastline, lighthouses, seabirds, seals, its traditional and unsophisticated agriculture, the profusion of wild orchids, the two churches and the Manor House contribute to its unique beauty. The National Trust displayed fine judgement in adding Fair Head and Murlough Bay to its properties. The magnificent proud headland, which divides sea and ocean, and its delightful neighbouring amphitheatre are attractive jewels.

Glenariff is fully deserving of the title "Queen of the Glens" not only because of its size but also for the grandeur of the cliffs that flank the glen. Over these cliffs flow tall waterfalls and the cascades within the upper reaches of the Glen are enjoyed by many tourists. The Garron Plateau is the most extensive area of upland blanket bog in Northern Ireland. Its multitudinous acres of bogland, interspersed with mountain lakes, are rarely visited. This sodden, apparently desolate, ground provides wide-open spaces, solitude, the occasional grouse, duck, heron, golden plover and hare. Some of its lakes have trout. Rare plants grow in unpolluted territory. Above all it offers peace and solitude.

Flowering Currant

Violets

Mayflower

Reeds in Craigmacagan Lough, Rathlin

Rocky Inlet, Rathlin

Glenariff in Snow

Gerard Manley Hopkins may never have visited Garron but he captured the spirit of the place when he wrote the following lines in his poem, *Inversnaid*:

"What would the world be, once bereft
Of wet and of wildness? Let them be left,
O let them be left, wildness and wet;
Long live the weeds and the wilderness yet."

Ushet Lough, Rathlin

The Coast Road is just as beautiful as Thackeray described it many years ago. It skirts the sea from Larne to Cushendall and continues inland to Cushendun and from there the traveller has a choice of two routes to Ballycastle. The vistas of headlands, hills, beaches, cliffs, the distant Scottish islands and mainland and the ever-changing sea and sky are glorious to behold.

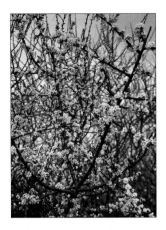

Blackthorn

Whin

when fully implemented will surely complement the Castle, the forest, the stock of fine old houses and the narrow streets. Carnlough, with its harbour and the Londonderry Arms Hotel, is a popular stopping place. Red Bay at the foot of Glenariff, under the shelter of Lurigedan and Carn Neill, has a superb sandy beach. Through the Red Arch in the town of Cushendall, Lurigedan dominates the skyline and there are distant views of Tievebulliagh and Carn Neill. The bay, the beach and the river contribute to the scene. Cushendun has a unique charm with its Maud cottages, shingle beach, bridge and river.

On a journey north Ballygally's sandy beach and the Castle Hotel in a picturesque setting have long been attractive to tourists. Glenarm's potential is yet to be fulfilled but the improvements to the harbour area

The traveller is now faced with a choice of routes. The main one lies over the hills past Loughareema and Ballypatrick Forest but the more scenic route lies closer to the sea. The narrow road to Torr Head and Fair Head

Ballycastle Beach and Fair Head

switchbacks and twists through the rugged coastal scenery. At the northern end of either route lies the large town of Ballycastle. The beach, with Fair Head as a backdrop, is the most expansive stretch of sand in the Glens. Ferries sail between the harbour and Rathlin. The rounded Knocklayde overlooks the town. This journey, or its reverse, is a most delightful blend of sea and land and its beauty is rarely equalled.

These features (Rathlin, Fair Head and Murlough Bay, Glenariff, the Garron plateau, the Coast Road) together with the archaeological remains and rich wildlife are to me the most precious sights in the landscape of the Glens.

Waterfall in Glenariff

Fair Head from Torr Head

Spindrift on Lough Doo

Seals on the Shore

1. Ballyconagan
2. Breen Wood
3. Carnanmore
4. Carnfunnock
5. Cushleake
6. Glenariff
7. Green Hill
8. Kebble
9. Murlough Bay
10. Portaleen Bay
11. Slievenahanaghan
12. Waterfoot

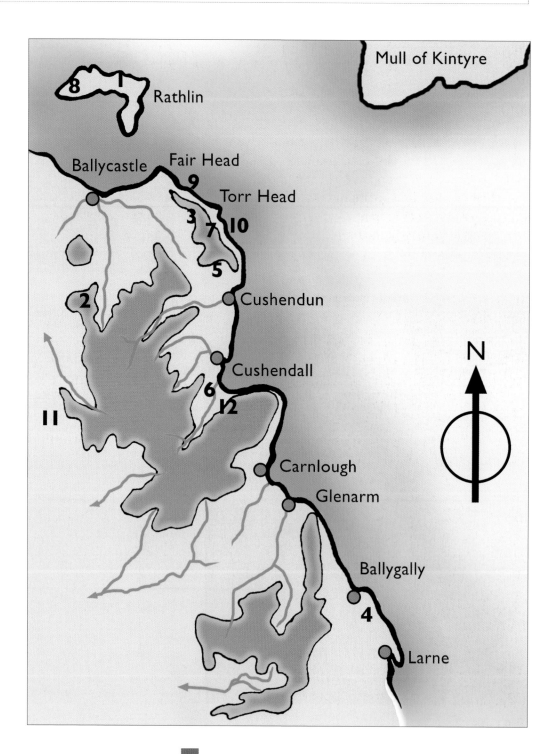

CHAPTER 8

FACING THE FUTURE

THE GLENS of Antrim are a rich inheritance but they cannot, and should not, be preserved as they are today. We need to protect the best features of the landscape while allowing change to take place. It is only by looking at the challenges that we can see how the Glens may best be managed for the benefit of residents, visitors and future generations.

The landowners

Some owner claims every acre of the Glens, through inheritance or purchase. But there is a larger question. Who really owns the Glens? Many centuries ago the easy answer was the McDonnells. The easy answer today is the totality of the landowners. But do they

Gate on Garron

own the majesty of the cliffs, the wildlife, the rarely-seen views, the splendour of the boggy uplands? Do they own the natural beauty of this designated Area of Outstanding Natural Beauty? Yes. They are the legal owners of their lands but they are also custodians for the rest of us who admire this precious region.

The Commission on the Future of Farming and Food reported in January 2002 that some subsidies would be directed towards the protection of the countryside. Some farmers would in future be rewarded for being countryside stewards rather than producers of food. As custodians they should be recompensed for maintaining their land in a manner that enhances the landscape. They should be encouraged (if encouragement be needed) to allow controlled access to those who wish to explore the Glens. Farmers' concerns regarding public liability need to be allayed. Grants to farmers for maintenance of the landscape and for permitting access would be in the interest of farmers and the public. In turn the public must respect the farmers' livestock, fences and crops.

Farms in the Glens tend to be small and uneconomic with the result that today's fieldscape is changing again. Some hedges are being removed to make larger fields and in the less favourable hill territory, hedges are let run wild and are expanding into the fields. The wide-open acres of rundale grazing that ranged the hilltops are now almost completely fenced. Overgrazing on this and other marginal land has led to encroachment of rushes and bracken. The intensive rearing of poultry and pigs leads to farmers building immense sheds. With carefully-chosen colours and well-selected positioning of these sheds their impact is minimised and most farmers are to be commended for this.

Rising costs and falling prices together with BSE and foot-and-mouth disease have been massive blows for the farming community. The resultant fall in tourist numbers caused by foot-and-mouth disease caused further hurt to those farmers who offered bed-and-breakfast accommodation or provided holiday homes to supplement farm incomes. Pressures are mounting for a reappraisal of farming and the use of subsidies to support what have become inappropriate agricultural practices across Europe. Hopefully this reappraisal will be seen as an opportunity for farmers to generate income by new means.

No matter what happens the importance of the involvement of farmers in creating the landscape of the Glens can't be ignored. The results of a landscape without farm animals could be seen all too clearly when foot and mouth disease caused temporary local havoc in infected areas in 2001 when fields were emptied of livestock and the countryside was strangely still. No lambs bleated; no calves ran in the fields. The sight of sheep and cattle peacefully grazing adds to the pastoral beauty of the Glens, part of what makes them the special place they are.

Northern Ireland has lagged behind the Republic of Ireland and England in the provision of rights of way. The first local legislation, Access to the Countryside Order (Northern Ireland), of 1983, required each District Council to "compile and preserve maps and other records of public rights of way in its district." Councils responsible for the Glens have dragged their feet with regard to this requirement (apart from the creation and maintenance of the Ulster and Moyle Ways) and implementation would surely encourage more visitors and open up the less well-known areas of the Glens.

JOHANN
Sculpted by
DEBORAH BROWN
and presented by her to
the people of Cushendun
August 2002
a goat was the last animal
to be culled in
the foot and mouth outbreak
spring 2001.

Foot and Mouth Memorial, by Deborah Brown

Housing and other features

New housing built to accommodate displaced agricultural workers, the expanding population and those who wish to move to the Glens, has been concentrated in the existing towns and villages. The beauty and comparative solitude of the Glens encourages new housing but creates threats to the landscape. For example, the expansion of the villages of Glenariff and Waterfoot has encroached on Glenariff Glen. How much of the Glen should be sacrificed to new housing before its character is irreparably damaged?

In 1808 a massive fort 420 feet in diameter was levelled in Newtown-Crommelin. Despite such a documented loss and many unrecorded losses, the Glens have a rich archaeological legacy. Superstition, or respect for the past, has helped preserve at least some of the megaliths. Others have escaped the notice of the Ordnance Survey mappers and some have yet to be rediscovered, perhaps in thickets of gorse, under a layer of bog or submerged in the sea. Archaeologists have uncovered some of the past of Glencloy but much of the archaeology of the Glens has yet to be explored and recorded. Hopefully the era of pilfering stone from archaeological sites to use in erecting walls or as part of a land clearance has come to an end and our appreciation and respect for the past will continue to grow and thus preserve these marvellous remnants of earlier millennia.

The restoration of abandoned cottages for the use of visitors has a long way to go to take full advantage of the fine settings of these ancient homesteads. Compared to Donegal, the number of holiday homes in the Glens is not as yet a serious problem. However the increasing number of static caravans is a potential threat to the landscape in Carnlough and Ballycastle.

The modern circular church on the seafront in Carnlough is an example to follow for future Glens architecture: as a new building, it adds character and dignity to the existing stock of ecclesiastical buildings.

There is an increase in access for recreational boats with the provision of the marina in Ballycastle and several slipways along the coast. The redevelopment

St. John's, Carnlough

of the dilapidated Glenarm Harbour as a marina has added further boating facilities. The successful enterprise of Red Bay Boats has encouraged greater boat ownership and opened opportunities for excursions to the Scottish islands.

Another change on the coast has been the introduction of salmon cages off Glenarm and Red Bay and these are now well-established. The enterprise provides employment in its river-based hatchery and in the farming, harvesting and processing of the fish. The predictable and controllable provision of farmed salmon (except when the cages are breached) has helped counterbalance the rapidly declining stocks of wild fish, although some argue that such farming has adversely affected the wild salmon population.

To drive the winding Coast Road on a quiet winter's day is a pleasure. The same road on a sunny Sunday in summer provides a completely different experience. Because there is little opportunity for safe overtaking, traffic moves at the frustrating pace of the slowest driver. As the number of vehicles on all roads has increased, so has the traffic of the Glens. Heavy commercial vehicles do not fit comfortably on roads that were designed for the horse-drawn traffic of many years ago. Will these narrow roads be adequate for future traffic?

Salmon Cages in Red Bay

If the proportion of visitors to locals is relatively low, then a holiday area can usually cope comfortably and enjoy the tourists and the business they generate. When the proportion of visitors is high, there is a danger that the character of the locality will be distorted. Rathlin must be close to that stage – especially with the provision of the improved ferry service and with a resident population of around one hundred.

It is important for communities to have access to electricity, telephones and television. However, the accompanying masts, poles, wind turbines, overhead cables, aerials and satellite dishes, when they are obtrusively sited, detract enormously from the landscape.

This is especially so when a structure impinges on the skyline as in the case of mobile phone and television masts at Glenarm. Poles and wires also dominate the summit at the Standing Stone on the Mullaghsandall Road (north of Larne) where an apparent lack of planning has resulted in there being two sets of parallel electricity lines. It is costly to put right the existing state of affairs but tighter controls on new developments may help to lessen their impact.

Sadly one of the threats to this changing and potentially idyllic area is the preponderance of litter. Consumer society encourages disposal rather than repair, and enfolds new products in multitudinous layers of wrapping. These factors and careless people have led to increasing amounts of litter. Despite the efforts of local councils in weekly collection of household refuse and the provision of facilities for the easy disposal of rubbish, litter blights the landscape. It is amazing that some people drive to quiet rural areas to discard items such as refrigerators, beds, settees, television sets and car batteries when they could simply drive to council refuse facilities. Look over a bridge into an otherwise delightful stream and you will see examples of such rubbish.

The hedgerows are strewn with papers, plastic bags, empty drinks containers, cigarette packets, fast-food packaging – much of which has been jettisoned from cars, most of the rest blown from who knows where. Black plastic sheets impaled on thorn hedges flap their shreds endlessly. Those who discard litter do not appreciate the beauty of our countryside and the precious nature of our heritage, the legacy for succeeding generations.

Vandalism at Mullaghsandall

Managing the landscape

For these issues to be addressed there needs to be an overall view of how the Glens might best be managed for the benefit of residents, visitors and future generations. As we will see in the next section there is unfortunately no comprehensive approach to managing the Glens landscape.

Farmers, residents, visitors, hoteliers, elected representatives, environmentalists, prospectors and a host of others know many aspects of the Glens. Some exploit the area for whatever short-term benefit can be had but most recognise the unique nature of the place and wish to preserve its best features.

It is difficult for individuals to have much say in the management of the landscape but thankfully government and other bodies have been conscious of the need to conserve the landscape.

As early as 1956 the Ulster Society for the Preservation of the Countryside proposed a National Park to include Green Hill, Portaleen Bay, Torr Head, Murlough Bay, Fair Head, Carnanmore, Cushleake and perhaps Cushendun and Cushendall. However, it was not until 1988 that the Antrim Coast and Glens was designated an Area of Outstanding Natural Beauty (AONB).

This welcome designation recognises the Glens as a national asset and aims to protect and improve the area for residents and visitors. More specifically the Department of the Environment with regard to the AONB "may formulate proposals for:

(a) conserving or enhancing the natural beauty or amenities of that area;

(b) conserving wildlife, historic objects or natural phenomena within it;

(c) promoting its enjoyment by the public; and

(d) providing or maintaining public access to it."

However there was no provision for the positive management of the Glens of Antrim. In 2002 Dermott Nesbitt, the Environment Minister at Stormont announced that he had commissioned a study on national parks in the province. The Mournes and the Giant's Causeway, as well as the Antrim Coast and Glens, will be considered. National park status would facilitate co-ordinated management and enhanced funding. We look forward to a positive outcome of this study with regard to the Glens.

Various government departments and agencies contribute to the Glens. For example, Ballycastle, Cushendun, Cushendall, Carnlough and Glenarm have been declared Conservation Areas in an attempt to preserve their unique identities. The remnants of the ancient oak forest at Breen Wood are a National Nature Reserve. The State Forests provide scenic routes, parking and picnic areas as in Ballypatrick. The Tourist Board encourages the provision of amenities for visitors. The Environment Service aims "to protect and conserve the natural and man-made environment and to promote its appreciation for the benefit of present and future generations." The Department of Agriculture through the provision of grants, advice and regulation influences the landscape. Much of the Glens has been designated an Environmentally Sensitive Area since 1989. This voluntary scheme encourages farmers to conserve the landscape rather than adopt intensive modern farming practices. The scheme has proved successful in conserving the scenic beauty, wildlife habitats and distinctive heritage features. Activity in hedge restoration and drystone walling is one example of the impact of the scheme. Another is the attempt to reintroduce choughs to the Antrim cliffs. Local farmers are encouraged to practice farming that is conducive to the lifestyle of the choughs. Farmers are recompensed for their additional costs and for the income they forego. An imaginative expansion of this scheme would not only improve the landscape but would also attract more visitors and provide additional employment and income.

Four district councils (Larne, Moyle, Ballymena and Ballymoney) exercise limited responsibilities for building control and environmental services, such as refuse collection. The largest part of the Glens is within Moyle and Larne District Councils' boundaries. These councils have put in place the only two way-marked trails through the Glens – the Ulster and the Moyle Ways. Both trails traverse some of the grandest scenery but at times take unexpected and lengthy deviations onto roads due to farmers' reluctance to give access.

In general, the local councils have not been pro-active in fulfilling their responsibility to provide access to the countryside but the awarding of grants as recompense to farmers is beyond their powers. However, with regard to other aspects of landscape, Larne Borough Council has developed the Country Park at Carnfunnock and part-funded, together with the European Commission, the renovation of Glenarm Harbour.

Glenarm Marina

Other organisations play a significant role in contributing to the welfare of the Glens. The National Trust manages properties at Fair Head, Murlough Bay, Cushleake Mountain, Cushendun and the Manor House and Ballyconagan (a traditional farm) in Rathlin. The Royal Society for the Protection of Birds cares for its reserve at Kebble, and oversees the neighbouring seastacks on Rathlin. The Ulster Architectural Heritage Society has published detailed accounts of the stock of buildings in the Glens and Rathlin. It actively encourages preservation of the best of the buildings.

When one considers the array of organisations that has an impact for good on the landscape of the Glens one cannot help but be favourably impressed. Nonetheless there is no co-ordinated positive management of the Glens of Antrim. For example, are the four local councils' policies in harmony with regard to provision of services? Do the various government agencies collaborate or do they operate independently and at times in conflict with each other? Do European policies integrate comfortably with policies implemented by local or national bodies? How are the activities of organisations such as the National Trust or RSPB integrated into the overall welfare of the Glens? How do local people have a say in the management of their Area of Outstanding Natural Beauty?

The wonderful heritage of the landscape of the Glens must be conserved in conjunction with the social, agricultural and commercial needs of residents and visitors. It would be advantageous to have a single body to co-ordinate, orchestrate and oversee the Glens: this will be explored in the next section.

The Glens have long been relatively remote from major change and hopefully that will continue to be the case.

On this basis I will suggest several factors that are likely to influence the landscape of the Glens and then consider an ideal scenario for the future of the region.

Protecting the Glens

The first change referred to is a plan, rather than a forecast. It involves the current transformation of the village of Glenarm. The harbour improvements and the long overdue removal of the Whiting Mill will make the village more attractive to tourists. This in turn is likely to lead to renovations of properties, the provision of facilities to cater for tourists and pressure for additional housing. Glenarm will be revitalised as a result of these initiatives.

If the number of licences granted for oil and gas exploration is a reliable indicator then almost certainly there are rock structures containing fossil fuel in the Glens. Should a commercially viable deposit be found, the national economic argument in favour of fuel will be immense, yet there would probably be little local advantage other than a limited number of jobs. The rigs, pipeline and ancillary plant will provide disruption and will inevitably scar the Glens. Is this cost worthwhile?

Should wind farms prove to be cost effective, then it is likely that remote hilly areas such as the Glens will be attractive as a location for further installations. Rathlin needed its wind turbines to provide electricity but a proliferation in other regions of the Glens is undesirable. If Slievenahanaghan was deemed to be a suitable site for an experimental wind farm, what would stop there being further sites in the Glens – perhaps on even a larger scale?

Agriculture in the hill farms of the northern Glens is an increasingly threatened way of life. Small farmers need to generate income from other sources. This situation will worsen as subsidies are phased out. Despite the strong ties of tradition, more small farmers are going to have to face the decision as to whether or not to continue in agriculture. One asset, currently unexploited by the farmers and local councils, is the potential number of walkers who could be attracted to the Glens. Grants to assist the provision of access, stiles, secure car parking, accommodation (including campsites and barns) and cafes could provide additional income and open up regions hitherto unavailable to the public. However, the success of such enterprises depends on fulsome support from walkers and their willingness to pay for the provided facilities.

Tourism in the Glens is likely to increase. The rugged terrain, the Coast Road, the waterfalls, the lacework stone walls, the farms and the unsullied beauty will continue to appeal to tourists. The region has already seen an increase in the provision for tourism and this in turn will attract more visitors. There will however be a limit due to the restrictions of the infrastructure. We saw earlier how the lack of roads hindered contact between the Glens and the rest of Ulster until the Coast Road was built. The provision of new roads is unlikely and the narrow Coast Road will remain narrow for the foreseeable future. Traffic congestion and its management need to be addressed.

Lessons from the Lake District

As we have seen, the Glens lack a single unified approach to its management. There is no one organisation that people can recognise as having the overall welfare of the Glens as its primary function. My wish for the future would be to see the evolution of such a body. It has been done in other places and if we look to the highly successful Lake District in Cumbria we may learn from that experience. The Friends of the Lake District was established in 1934 to protect and conserve the area. Pressure from the Friends led to the establishment of the Lake District National Park in 1951. The UK Government and the European Union contribute substantial funding each year to managing the National Park. The vision of the Park Authority is: "It will be a place for all that can still inspire a sense of wonder and a feeling of freedom, engendered by an absence of unwarranted supervision and control, with ample opportunities to get away from crowds and unnecessary noise. It will be an area in which the private car has its necessary place but does not dominate; where pollution, in the widest sense of the word, does not spoil the environment or threaten people's well-being or enjoyment; and where all are aware of, appreciate and respond to the Park's value and vulnerability." Such a vision for the Glens of Antrim would be most desirable.

More specifically, the Park Authority has expressed a summary of its objectives. These are reproduced below with 'the Glens of Antrim' replacing the 'Lake District' and 'the National Park'.

Conservation of the Natural Environment:

"Conserve and enhance the diversity of landscapes throughout the Glens of Antrim, giving very high regard to the distinctive character of individual places, and the areas defined as important habitats. Protect those habitats and features that are irreplaceable, or are of special local significance. Press the case for support to retain traditional farm units.

Conservation of the Cultural Heritage:

"Protect and enhance nationally designated archaeological and cultural sites, historic and listed buildings. Ensure the resources are committed to the protection and enhancement of archaeological and historic features of local significance. Provide interpretative material, arrange events, and attend local shows to encourage greater interest in local cultural traditions. Encourage and promote Conservation Area Enhancement Schemes.

Recreation Management:

"Promote and manage access to the Glens of Antrim and maintain the footpaths and other rights of way. Support recreation that ensures the qualities of its landscape, wildlife and cultural heritage are maintained, and that does not spoil the enjoyment of others or disrupt the activities of the local community. Safeguard and enhance opportunities for the quiet enjoyment of the Glens of Antrim. Pursue suitable opportunities to extend access for quiet enjoyment and consider the needs of disabled people.

Promoting Understanding and Enjoyment:

"Instil an awareness of the need for conservation of the Glens of Antrim and an understanding of its special qualities. Encourage people to explore and enjoy the Glens in ways which do not spoil it for others, which conserve it for future generations, and respect that it is a living, working countryside. Inform people about its attractions and facilities and how they can enjoy the Glens of Antrim in safety.

Traffic and Transport:

"Promote the development and use of attractive alternative means of travel to the private motor vehicle and generally reduce the adverse impact of motor traffic on the environment and on the enjoyment and well being of residents and visitors. Manage off road driving in the Glens."

These, or similar objectives, for the Glens of Antrim would help ensure that current and future generations would continue to enjoy a landscape that is inspirational and delightful. With the creation of a National Park there would be one readily identifiable body responsible for the Glens. There would be representation of local people and organisations in the management of the Glens. There would be a budget and additional funds solely for the enhancement of the area

In the long-term our guiding principle has to be to conserve what is good so that future generations will benefit from this and bless, not curse, us. The creation of a National Park for the Antrim Coast and Glens would help achieve this goal.

Let us not forget that Nature still has her part to play even if imperceptibly. Mudslides, the gradual slippage of the coastal hills as at Garron Point, rock fall at Fair Head and further coastal erosion by the sea will continue to shape our landscape. Rising sea levels attributable to global warming may inundate the Coast Road and put coastal housing at risk. Flora, fauna and the crops grown may change as weather patterns change. Nature will have her say! We live in a dynamic world where we have inherited the multi-faceted beauty of the Antrim Coast and Glens. Let us cherish them and do our best to allow our descendants to know what we have known.

Appendix – The Science Of Archaeology

1. Archaeological evidence from organic materials

How do we date stone artefacts? As we saw in Chapter 1, it is possible to find the age of a stone from its uranium or iron oxides content. This is of no use to us in ascertaining when man worked the stone. It is only when the stone is found in context with organic materials that it is possible to identify when it became a tool or weapon or building material.

Much of the organic material that Mesolithic man used in Ireland has perished. Archaeologists would be delighted to find a relatively intact site with wooden items, clothing, houses and other artefacts in a reasonable state of preservation. However, even with meagre scraps of organic evidence, scientists have used several approaches to estimate the age of archaeological discoveries.

Radio carbon dating. Carbon 14 is found in all living organisms. After death, organisms absorb no further carbon 14 and the amount already absorbed decays slowly and at a constant rate over a lengthy period. By measuring the amount still in existence in a sample from cremated or burnt bones, archaeologists can determine reasonably accurately the period when the human or animal was alive. A sample pig vertebra from Mount Sandel could indicate with 95% probability that the pig had been alive between 6900 and 6500 BC. Any surviving organic material or remains may be dated by this means.

Osteoarchaeology is the study of human and animal bones found in excavated sites. Sometimes complete skeletons are unearthed but usually analysis has to be done on single bones or pieces of bone. Where our ancestors practised cremation, remnants of the skull or teeth often survived. Pelvic bones help determine gender, as do the size and shape of the skull and the long bones from legs or arms. Until about the age of twenty-five human teeth and bones develop at a relatively uniform rate. Beyond that age, the body starts to degenerate. On this basis archaeologists are able to roughly estimate the age at which our ancestors died. They can also show from the study of bones, that early man suffered from arthritis and had many dental problems caused by tooth cavities. Current research in this area involves the extraction of DNA from bones for more detailed analysis to provide further information on the past.

Pollen analysis provides evidence as to what plants grew most profusely. Pollen carries the male genetic material of flowering plants. Pollen dust settles in layers on lakes and peat bogs. The grains of pollen are remarkably indestructible and the grains of each plant species are unique. When scientists extract a core from the bottom of lakes or peat bogs this core gives a record of pollen over many years of plant activity. The dating of the layers in the sample core is done by radiocarbon analysis as discussed earlier. It has been possible to go back 13,000 years in Ireland and to trace the early evolution from grassland to forest and the subsequent decline of the forest.

It is common knowledge that we can calculate the age of a freshly felled tree by counting the rings. The varying widths of rings also provide evidence of good and poor growing seasons and of long term climatic change. **Dendrochronology** is the scientific study of this phenomenon and the Queen's University of Belfast has been at the international forefront of this work. The most useful trees for this study are those that provide durable timber. Oak is best in this respect because it has long been used in building and we can also get samples from bog-oak.

We would expect two trees of similar age to have similar growth rings. If we have two trees whose lifespans overlap then at least some of their growth rings should be the same. Using this principle it is possible to chain backwards and at Queen's University there is now a template that enables timber up to 7,000 years old to be dated.

2. Other scientific methods used by archaeologists

When the earth has been disturbed as in the building of walls, ditches or the making of fires, the magnetic balance of the soil changes. Even though there is no evidence on the surface of such activity due, for example, to intensive ploughing, it is possible to use a **magnetometer** to identify such changes. This device is used when walking in a regular pattern over the surface. Its output is used to produce maps of changes in magnetism beneath the surface. This in turn assists the archaeologist to decide where and how extensively to dig.

Aerial photography reveals features not visible from the ground. These occur in, for example, a barley field where a circular enclosure has previously existed. The disturbed soil has different characteristics and the different growth rates of the barley reveal a pattern that may be best viewed from the sky. The analysis is based on the differing heights of stalks not as in crop circles where the stalks have been flattened.

Unsuspected lazy beds are often visible in morning or evening light when the long shadows cast by the sun display the ribbed pattern in a field. Similarly other bumps and hollows cast shadows, especially when photographed from an aircraft in low winter sunshine when vegetation is minimal. Many previously undiscovered archaeological sites have been found by this method.

The following "aerial photograph" is taken from the cliffs in Glenariff and it illustrates the power of this method. Low winter sun picks out the lazy beds – some straight, some curved because of the obstruction of a more ancient mound with indentation and an accompanying dyke. The re-distribution of land and the new field boundaries are shown by the disruption of the curved lazy beds with the newer stone dyke and fence. Three distinct patterns of the past in one image!

Historical Patterns in the Landscape

BIBLIOGRAPHY

Aalen, F.H.A., K. Whelan and M. Stout, *Atlas of the Rural Irish Landscape*, Cork University Press, 1997.

Antrim Coast and Glens, Area of Outstanding Natural Beauty, Guide to Designation, Department of the Environment for Northern Ireland, HMSO, 1988.

Bardon, J., *A History of Ulster*, Blackstaff, 1992.

Boyd, H.A., 'Ancient Cross na Naghan in Layde Churchyard, Cushendall', *The Glynns* (Journal of the Glens of Antrim Historical Society), Vol. 3, 1975.

Boyd, H.A., 'Dean William Henry's Topographical Description of the Coast of County Antrim and North Down around 1740', *The Glynns*, Journal of the Glens of Antrim Historical Society, Vol. 3, 1975.

Brett, C.E.B., *Historic Buildings, Groups of Buildings, Areas of Architectural Importance in the Glens of Antrim*, Ulster Architectural Heritage Society, 1971.

Brett, C.E.B., *Historic Buildings, Groups of Buildings, Areas of Architectural Importance in the Island of Rathlin*, Ulster Architectural Heritage Society, 1974.

Brett, C.E.B., *Five Big Houses of Cushendun and Some Literary Associations*, Lagan Press, 1997.

Capper, W., *Caring for the Countryside, A History of 50 Years of the Ulster Society for the Preservation of the Countryside*, Ulster Society for the Preservation of the Countryside, 1988.

Carmody, W.P., *Cushendall and its Neighbourhood – A Guide*, Browne & Nolan, 1904.

Carter, B., *Shifting Sands: A Study of the Coast of Northern Ireland from Magilligan to Larne*, HMSO, 1991.

Case, H. 'Settlement Patterns in the North Irish Neolithic', *Ulster Journal of Archaeology*, Vol. 32, 1969.

Charlesworth, J.K., *The Geology of Ireland*, Oliver and Boyd, 1966.

Clark, W., *Rathlin, Its Island Story*, Impact Printing, 1995.

Dallat, C. (compiler) *McCahan's Local Histories, a Series of Pamphlets of North Antrim and the Glens* (1923), The Glens of Antrim Historical Society, 1988.

Dallat, C., *Antrim Coast and Glens – A Personal View*, HMSO, 1990.

De Latocnaye, *A Frenchman's Walk Through Ireland, 1796-97*, The Blackstaff Press, 1984.

Delaney, F., *The Celts*, Grafton Books, 1989.

Diamond, J., *Guns, Germs and Steel - A Short History of Everybody for the Last 13,000 Years*, Vintage, 1998.

Dobbs, R.S., 'Statistical Account of Ardclinis and Laid', *The Glynns*, Journal of the Glens of Antrim Historical Society, Vol. 1, 1973.

Donnelly, C.J., *Living Places*, The Institute of Irish Studies, The Queen's University of Belfast, 1997.

Ellis, P.E., *Celtic Inheritance*, Constable, 1992.

Environmental Resources Management, *Northern Ireland Landscape Character Assessment 2000, An Appreciation and Analysis of the Landscape of the Region*, Corporate Document Service, 2001.

Evans, E.E., *The Personality of Ireland: Habitat, Heritage and History*, Belfast, 1981.

Gallagher, L. and Rogers, D., *Castle, Coast and Cottage – The National Trust in Northern Ireland*, Blackstaff Press, 1992.

From Glynn to Glen (a visual record of a millenium), Glens of Antrim Historical Society, 2000.

Guide to the Glens of Antrim, The Causeway Coast and Antrim Glens Ltd, 2005.

Halstead, L.B., *Hunting the Past*, Hamish Hamilton, 1982.

Hamlin, A. and C. Lynn, *Pieces of the Past, Archaeological Excavations by the Department of the Environment for Northern Ireland 1970-1986*, HMSO, Belfast, 1988.

Gaston, R. and O. McGilloway, *Gaston's Glynnes*, The Arches Art Gallery, 1994.

Hammond, F., *Antrim Coast and Glens Industrial Heritage*, HMSO, 1991.

Harper, D., 'Kelp Burning in the Glens', *The Glynns*, Journal of the Glens of Antrim Historical Society, Vol. 3, 1975.

Herity, M. and G. Eogan, *Ireland in Prehistory*, Routledge and Kegan Paul, 1977.

Herity, M. *Irish Passage Graves*, Irish University Press, 1974.

Hewitt, J. and C. McAuley, *The Day of the Corncrake, Poems of the Nine Glens by John Hewitt and Paintings by Charles McAuley*, The Glens of Antrim Historical Society, 1984.

Hill, G., *An Historical Account of the MacDonnells of Antrim*, Archer and Sons, 1873.

Hodges, R., 'Knockdhu Promontory Fortress: An interpretation of its function in the light of some preliminary fieldwork', *Ulster Journal of Archaeology*, Vol. 38, 1975.

Irvine, J. 'Carnlough Harbour Development Scheme 1854-64', *The Glynns* (Journal of the Glens of Antrim Historical Society), Vol. 5, 1977.

Irvine, J. 'The Campletown Customs Records', *The Glynns* (Journal of the Glens of Antrim Historical Society), Vol. 4, 1976.

Jope, E.M., 'Porcellanite Axes from Factories in North-East Ireland: Tievebulliagh and Rathlin', *Ulster Journal of Archaeology*, Vol. 15, Parts 1 and 2, 1952.

Knowles, W.J., 'Stone Axe Factories near Cushendall', *Royal Society of Antiquaries of Ireland*, Vol. 36, 1906.

Lutgens, F.K. and E.J. Tarbuck, *Essentials of Geology*, Charles E. Merrill, 1982.

Lynn, C.J., 'Houses in Rural Ireland AD 500-1000', *Ulster Journal of Archaeology*, 3rd Series, Vol. 57, 1994.

Lynn, C.J. and J.A. McDowell, 'A Note on the Excavation of an Early Christian Period Settlement in Deer Park Farms, Glenarm – 1984-1987', *The Glynns* (Journal of the Glens of Antrim Historical Society), Vol. 16, 1988.

Mallory, J.P., and T.E. McNeill, *The Archaeology of Ulster*, The Institute of Irish Studies, The Queen's University of Belfast, 1991.

Marshall, J.D.C., *Forgotten Places of the North Coast*, Clegnagh Publishing, 1991.

McBride, J., *Traveller in the Glens*, Appletree Press, 2004.

McDonnell, H., 'Glenarm Friary and the Bissets', *The Glynns* (Journal of the Glens of Antrim Historical Society), Vol. 15, 1987.

McKavanagh, P., 'Penal Mass Sites in the Glens', *The Glynns*, Journal of the Glens of Antrim Historical Society, Vol. 1, 1973.

McKillop, F., *Glenarm, A Local History*, Ulster Journals Ltd., 1987.

McKillop, F., *Glencloy, A Local History*, Ulster Journals Ltd., 1996.

McQuillan, P., *The Tenth Glen and Other Ballads*, Impact Printing, 1978.

McNeill, L. 'The Sulphate of Ammonia Company Limited – Carnlough', *The Glynns* (The Journal of the Glens of Antrim Historical Society) Vol. 8, 1980.

Mitchell, F. and M. Ryan, *Reading the Irish Landscape*, Town House, Dublin, 1997.

Movius, H.J., *The Irish Stone Age*, Cambridge, 1942.

O'Corrain, D., *Milestones in Irish History*, edited by Liam de Paor, Mercier Press, 1986.

O'Neill, M., *Songs of the Glens of Antrim*, Blackwood & Sons, 1933.

Ordnance Survey Memoirs of Ireland, Parishes of County Antrim Vol. 10, III, Larne and Islandmagee, The Institute of Irish Studies, The Queen's University of Belfast, 1991.

Ordnance Survey Memoirs of Ireland, Parishes of County Antrim Vol. 13, IV, Glens of Antrim, The Institute of Irish Studies, The Queen's University of Belfast, 1992.

Ordnance Survey Memoirs of Ireland, Parishes of County Antrim Vol. 24, IX, North Antrim Coast and Rathlin, The Institute of Irish Studies, The Queen's University of Belfast, 1993.

Ormsby, F. (Ed.), *The Collected Poems of John Hewitt*, Blackstaff Press, 1991.

Patterson, E.M., *The Ballymena Lines*, David & Charles, 1968.

Perceval-Maxwell, M., *The Scottish Migration to Ulster in the Reign of James I*, Routledge & Keegan Paul, 1990.

Pfeiffer, W. and M. Shaffrey, *Irish Cottages*, Weidenfeld & Nicolson, 1990.

Powell, T.G.E., *The Celts*, Thames and Hudson, 1980.

Praeger, R.L., *The Way That I Went*, Hodges, Figgis & Co. Ltd., 1947.

Proudfoot, V.B., and T.D. Vaughan, 'Changes in Settlement and Population in Northern Ireland, 1835-1860', *Ulster Folklife*, Vol. 5, 1959.

Rhodes, D., *A Wreath of Song*, Esson Publishers, 2004.

Robinson, P., 'The Ulster Plantation, in The Shaping of the Ulster Landscape', *A Publication of the Federation for Ulster Local Studies*, Vol. 11, Number 2, Winter 1989.

Sidebotham, J.M., 'A Settlement in Goodland Townland, Co. Antrim', *Ulster Journal of Archaeology*, Vol. 13, Parts 1 and 2, 1950.

Smith, A.G., *Neolithic and Bronze Age landscape changes in Northern Ireland*,

Smith, B. and P. Warke, *Classic Landforms of the Antrim Coast*, Geographical Association, 2001.

Walker, B.M., *Faces of the Past*, Appletree Press, 1974.

Williams, M. and D. Harper, *The Making of Ireland – Landscapes in Geology*, Immel Publishing, 1999.

Wilson, H.E., *Regional Geology of Northern Ireland*, HMSO, 1972.

Woodman, P.C., *The Mesolithic in Ireland*, BAR British Series 58, Oxford, 1978.

Other Sources:

Carleton, T., Series of lectures on Rocks and Landscape, The Queen's University of Belfast outcentre at Whitehead, Spring 2001.

Carleton, T., Series of lectures on the Ulster landscape, The Queen's University of Belfast, Spring 2000.

Kennan, P., *Written in Stone*, a television series produced by RTE, Dublin.

The Lake District National Park Authority website: www.lake-district.gov.uk

Woodman, P.C., *From Stone to Stone – 10,000 years in the Life of an Antrim Glen*, An Ulster Television production, Belfast, 1987.

ACKNOWLEDGEMENTS

FIRSTLY I thank Appletree Press for providing the opportunity for this work to be published. Jean Brown, my editor, and John Murphy, Managing Director, were supportive and helpful to me in many ways. I would also like to thank Appletree Press for allowing me to use quotations from their books, *The Traveller in the Glens* by Jack McBride and *The Little Book of Celtic Wisdom* compiled by Sean McMahon.

I owe much to the Glens of Antrim Rambling Club for introducing me, over many years, through their leaders and walks to the less well-known beauties of the Glens as well as the obvious highlights. Seamus Delargy, Peter King, Kaye Aicken and Pat McGregor have provided lively company in further explorations. More recently the formation of Wesley's Walkers has given me the opportunity to introduce others to the Glens. Their appreciation of the landscape has further kindled my interest.

Peter King read and appraised an early draft of the text. I appreciate the time he has given to this and acknowledge fully his useful recommendations and the improvements that have resulted.

Cahal Dallat kindly agreed to read a later version and he gave me considerable encouragement and support for which I am most grateful. I was exceptionally pleased (because of his great knowledge of, and love for, the Glens) that he agreed to write the foreword.

Several series of lectures by Trevor Carleton (on landscape) and Jim Mallory (on archaeology) of the Institute of Lifelong Learning of the Queen's University of Belfast were inspirational and contributed immensely to my knowledge. An enthusiastic Steve Balek accompanied me to these lectures and on several exploratory expeditions.

To all the landowners on whose ground I have walked – thank you! You are guardians of a wonderful heritage that I have been privileged to share.

Trevor Gibb of the East Antrim Institute introduced me to the basic skills of photography while Colin McIlwaine, Geraldine Gallagher and fellow members of Image 10+ have helped me hone those skills. Geraldine provided further help by using her graphic designer's skills in producing a first draft for Appletree Press.

I am also grateful to Blackstaff Press who gave permission to use quotations from John Hewitt's beautiful poems. These were all taken from the *Collected Poems of John Hewitt*, edited by Frank Ormsby and published by Blackstaff Press in 1991. The poems are reproduced by permission of Blackstaff Press on behalf of the Estate of John Hewitt.

Finally to my wife, Maureen, I offer thanks for the fulsome support she has given me in writing and illustrating this book.